M000266875

For my Mother
Mrs. Eleanor "Bay" Thomas

Contents

Acknowledgments

There are not any worthy accomplishments that are achieved alone. With this thought in mind, I am indebted to those individuals who have provided encouragement and words of wisdom on my career path to the university presidency. I thank Freeman Hrabowski, president of the University of Maryland Baltimore County, for his guidance, support, and mentorship, and for allowing me to shadow him as an American Council on Education Fellow (ACE Fellow). I thank Dolores Spikes, retired president of the University of Maryland Eastern Shore and president emeritus of Southern University Baton Rouge for her support as I rose through the ranks in higher education, for her mentorship, and for providing me with various opportunities and experiences that aided me in being a successful administrator. I want to thank Sidney McPhee, president of Middle Tennessee State University, for believing in me and for his guidance. In addition, I thank Al Goldfarb, president emeritus of Western Illinois University for having confidence in me as his provost and academic vice president. Al has been a great mentor and friend. All of these individuals have been instrumental in my growth and development as a president.

I thank my family and friends for their support. I am grateful for my wife Linda's undying support, which has allowed me to pursue my dreams. I am thankful for my sons Patrick and Darius, for I am proud to watch you develop into great young men, but there are still goals to obtain and still greatness to be achieved. Sons, stay the course. I thank my extended family in Alabama. In particular, I thank my father Clinton Thomas, Sr., my sister Helen Thomas Bell, and my brother, Marshall Clifford Thomas. I thank you all for your unwavering support.

Finally, I want to dedicate this book in memory of my mother, Eleanor "Bay" Cook Thomas, who passed away before I could finish writing it. My mother told me at an early age that she wanted me to finish high school and go to college, and that someone had to do something different from what she and my father had done. It is because of my mother's encouragement that I went to college and was a first-generation college student. My mother passed away on December 27, 2013, of Alzheimer's. I also want to dedicate this book in memory of my brother,

Clinton "June" Thomas, Jr., who financed my freshman year of studies. I am who I am because of my family. "Mama, I did what you told me to do."

I thank the members of my staff at Western Illinois University, who continually pushed me to "work on the book" and to "get the book done." I therefore thank Margaritta Fields, Kerry McBride, Paula Rhodes, and Christi Reed. I also wish to thank all those who read drafts of this work and provided suggestions to make this a better book. In particular, I thank Erik Brooks, Ron Williams, Al Goldfarb, Gloria Bonner, Janice Lewis, and many others for their support.

Author Information

Dr. Jack Thomas was named the eleventh president of Western Illinois University on January 18, 2011, and began his presidential tenure July 1, 2011. Dr. Thomas leads an institution that serves nearly 12,000 students through its traditional, residential four-year campus in Macomb, Illinois, and its metropolitan campus in the Quad Cities/Moline, Illinois. Western offers sixty-six undergraduate degree programs and thirty-eight graduate degree programs.

Under his leadership, Western Illinois University continues to be ranked as a "Best Midwestern College" and as a "Best Regional University" by The *Princeton Review and U.S. News and World Report*, respectively. During Dr. Thomas' tenure, numerous programs and initiatives have been established and improved, including increased partnerships with international universities and embassies, additional scholarship funding, the Western Commitment Scholarship, and the Centennial Honors College Scholarship programs, a mentoring program designed to improve retention, and an enhanced honors college. In addition, numerous academic programs have been established, highly selective and extraordinary signature academic programs have been identified, and Western's First Year Experience has undergone an extensive revision. Western Illinois University continues to improve its facilities under Dr. Thomas' guidance, including the renovation of the Three-Dimensional Art Facility, Corbin/Olson and Thompson residence halls, and science labs. Other projects on the Macomb Campus include the remodeling of the University Union, the installation of new turf on Hanson Field, and enhancement of the landscaping and lighting throughout the campus, which includes a new grand entrance to the campus. Through Western's beautification project, the Macomb campus was designated a Tree Campus USA by the Arbor Foundation. Under Dr. Thomas' leadership, Phase I of the Quad Cities Riverfront Campus has opened and Phase II is under construction.

Prior to his appointment as president, Dr. Thomas served as the University's provost and academic vice president from January 2008 through June 2011. Before joining the Western Illinois University administration, he served as senior vice provost for academic affairs and interim dean at Middle Tennessee State

University. Dr. Thomas has also served in various capacities at other universities, including interim president, executive vice president, associate vice president for academic and student affairs, executive assistant to the president, department chair, coordinator of freshman English, and assistant track coach. He is a graduate of the Harvard Leadership Program, and has been an American Council on Education Fellow and a Kellogg-NAFEO Fellow. Dr. Thomas is also a member of the following Boards: the Board of Trustees at Stillman College, the Board of the American Association of Blacks in Higher Education, and the Illinois Campus Compact. He has also served on the executive board for the American Council on Education Council of Fellows.

Dr. Thomas is the author of numerous scholarly publications, is a frequent presenter at professional conferences, is a noted lecturer, and is an invited keynote speaker for regional and national meetings and events. His research agenda focuses primarily on black males in literature, and he is the former editor and founder of "Image: The Scholars Release Journal, Men and Women of Color." As a strong proponent of mentoring young faculty from diverse backgrounds, Dr. Thomas has established underrepresented dissertation and postdoctoral fellowships, visiting professorships, young scholar initiatives, and other programs that support their professional development. He is a member of Alpha Phi Alpha, Sigma Pi Phi, Phi Kappa Phi, Sigma Tau Delta, and many other organizations. In the Macomb community, Dr. Thomas is a member of the Macomb Noon Rotary, and he is affiliated with the McDonough District Hospital's Golden Apple Society, the Performing Arts Society, Macomb Area Economic Development Corporation (MAEDCO), the Community and University Partnership Program (CUPP), and the Macomb Area Chamber of Commerce and Downtown Development Corporation.

A native of Lowndes County, Alabama, Dr. Thomas earned his Ph.D. from Indiana University of Pennsylvania, his master's degree from Virginia State University, and his bachelor's degree from Alabama A & M University. Dr. Thomas and his wife, Dr. Linda Thomas, have two sons, Patrick and Darius.

Preface

When people discover my occupation, I find myself answering three questions. Those early in their academic careers and who aspire to the university presidency often ask, "How can I become a university president?" Those who are in the middle of their careers and who know the pressures of being a university president ask, "How do you deal with the plethora of issues facing university presidents and universities?" Those outside the academy ask, "What exactly do you do as a university president?" This book is an attempt to answer those and many other questions that I have been asked over the years.

The title of the book was derived from the silent film entitled, *Within Our Gates,* written and produced and directed by groundbreaking filmmaker Oscar Micheaux during the 1900s. Micheaux is considered to be the first African American director of feature films. In the movie, the central character and heroine, Sylvia Landry, moves to the rural South and becomes employed as a teacher in a school for black children. When the school experiences financial problems, she goes to Boston to raise money for it. Though this film was controversial when it was released in 1919 because of its harsh, but truthful portrayal of the time, I thought it was fitting to incorporate its title into the title of my work.

In this book, I attempt to cover the aspects of the university presidency and discuss what happens or could happen "within the gates" of the academe. I use personal stories coupled with current happenings in higher education to discuss pertinent and relevant issues that academic leaders face, and hopefully shed some insight on these issues.

In chapter one, I discuss my own career path and trajectory to the university presidency. In chapter two, I discuss academic affairs as it pertains to the university presidency. In this chapter, I discuss how presidents are recruited and interviewed. I also discuss the knowledge, skills, and abilities needed to become a university president. I conclude this chapter by discussing curriculums, undergraduate, and graduate programs.

In chapter three, I discuss some of the key aspects of the presidency and public and community relations. The importance of various external relationships is expounded upon in this chapter, and it provides a critical understanding that developing relationships with the external community is a key to a success-ful presidency. In chapter four, I briefly examine organization theory as it relates to the university and discuss the various academic career positions that one may experience on the path to the university presidency.

In chapter five, I return to my faculty roots and discuss the faculty and the myriad of issues they may face. In this chapter, I discuss in general terms the fac-ulty hiring process and faculty tenure and promotion. Chapter six examines the various aspects of student affairs and the university presidency. In this chapter, I look at the university president and the relationship with students and various student groups.

Chapter seven reviews various issues with admissions and admissions poli-cies and how the use of technology has changed the admissions process. In chap-ter eight, I consider the presidency and the growth of intercollegiate athletics, and the tension that "big time" athletics can cause for some universities.

In chapter nine, I discuss religion on campuses and the university presi-dency. I also tackle racism, sexism, and LBGT issues as they pertain to university campuses. The concluding chapter of this book discusses the fish-bowl effect and other pressures that universities face. The chapter looks at various leadership pro-grams in which one could participate to prepare themselves for the presidency.

In this work, when I have provided examples and clarifications, I have at-tempted to use a wide range of examples. I have pulled from my knowledge of historically black colleges, predominately white colleges, large universities, small universities, religiously affiliated universities, and secular universities.

CHAPTER 1

The Personal Leadership Journey

At the age of twenty-three, I began my career in higher education as director of the writing center and English Instructor at Johnson C. Smith University (JSCU) in Charlotte, North Carolina. I enjoyed working with students and mentoring them. It was particularly easy to work with them because I was close to them in age. In fact, some students were older. Serving as director of the center gave my first experience as a leader in higher education. Even though it was an entry-level management position, it helped to shape my leadership style and it provided many opportunities and experiences. My leadership style is quite simple. I believe in involving individuals in decision making as much as possible by building consensus. Sometimes as a leader, one has to make decisions that are unpopular, or one has to make decisions at the spur of the moment. At a minimum, therefore, it is important to inform individuals of decisions that were made and why. When decisions are made, even if they are unpopular individuals will understand if they are involved in the decision-making process. Over the years, my leadership style has worked well, and it has helped me to grow and to progress.

Many people have perceived me to be younger than I am. This has hindered my progression toward senior-level leadership positions; however, many people believe that I have risen through the ranks sooner than many of my peers. I use to wear a suit and tie intentionally so I could be distinguished as a professional rather than a student. Based on the perceptions regarding my age, prior to being hired at JCSU, the chair of the English department gave me a long lecture about being a professional at all times. She told me that I absolutely could not date the students because I would lose credibility. She told me to do my job to the best of my ability, and that she would keep an eye on me at all times. After I was hired, she would stop by periodically to follow through on her promise. Once she got a chance to know me, however, she really began to put her trust in me. She then knew that I was a very serious individual who had good morals and values. I enjoyed my experiences at JCSU. My supervisor became like a mother and mentor to me as well as to others. It was a good nurturing environment. I stayed at JCSU for about three to four years.

I later interviewed for a position at South Carolina State College (SCSC). I was told that many individuals wanted an older person for the position; however, the dean of the school said that he wanted someone who was young, energetic, and able to relate to the students. I was the successful candidate, and I was hired as an English Instructor in the school of freshman studies to teach students who had writing deficiencies. After spending one semester at SCSC, I was awarded a fellowship to earn a Ph.D. in English at Indiana University of Pennsylvania. My dean, Dr. James Washington, Jr., told me that I should take the opportunity to earn my Ph.D. Dr. Washington fortunately granted me the opportunity to leave my position without pay while I earned my doctorate; therefore, upon completing the course work, I returned to SCSC to teach and write my dissertation. In May 1990, I graduated with a Ph. D. in English (Literature and Criticism). After the completion of my degree, I wanted to stay at SCSC; however, the vice president for academic affairs would not offer me an assistant professor position. Although Dean Washington requested that the college increase my rank to that of assistant professor, the request was ultimately denied and I moved on to accept an offer from another institution. After I carefully reviewed my options, I ultimately accepted a position as an assistant professor of English at the University of Maryland Eastern Shore.

I arrived at the University of Maryland Eastern Shore (UMES) in August 1990. At the time, UMES was a small institution with approximately 2,800 students. It was surrounded by a vast amount of farmland and open fields. In fact, the campus appeared to have been dilapidated. The various construction projects on the campus created dust when it was dry and mud when it was wet. The state had fortunately provided funds to do a total makeover of the campus. Although I had only planned to spend one year at UMES, I remained there for fourteen years. As a new assistant professor of English at UMES, I was very excited and I had vast amounts of energy, many ideas, and several goals to achieve. I had a good rapport with my students; however, some of them felt that my expectations were too high. I expected excellence at all levels, especially in the classroom. I was a stickler on grammar usage, and speaking correctly. As a black male, I always felt that I was being watched and held to the highest standards of the academy.

As time progressed, I was tenured and promoted to the rank of associate professor. It was only a few months later that I became the interim chair of the Department of English and Modern Languages. My hat is off to anyone who serves as a chair of a department, for it involves so many details. I was able to build consensus among the English and language faculty. After serving as Interim chair for about a year, I competed in a national search and became the chair of the Department of English and Modern Languages. I gained invaluable experience as chair because of the many facets of the position and the many challenges that arose. The chair is a midlevel position where an individual works with senior-level administrators, faculty, staff, and students. The key to being successful as a chairperson is to work well with all individuals and to keep the lines of communication open.

The new president, Dolores Spikes, asked me to apply for the American Council on Education Fellowship (ACE), which is an opportunity for individuals to gain intense experience learning about being an administrator. I had applied for the fellowship once before; however, I was told that I was not successful because I did not have administrative experience. Nevertheless, I was successful in obtaining the fellowship under President Spikes' recommendation and leadership. I was a member of the class of 1998–99. My classmates told me that I had the best placement, which was with Freeman Hrabowski, president of the University of Maryland Baltimore County (UMBC). President Hrabowski is arguably one of the most renowned college presidents in the country. I spent one semester in the president's office at UMBC which is a predominately white institution (PWI) led by its first African American president. I spent the second semester of the fellowship at my home institution, the University of Maryland Eastern Shore, with Spikes. President Spikes is a renowned African American female president who was the first woman to serve as president at UMES. While I was at UMBC, President Hrabowski helped to facilitate my travels to London and to various places in Europe as part of my fellowship and research. This was my first experience traveling abroad. While I was at UMES, during the second semester, President Spikes encouraged and supported me to enroll in the Salzburg Seminar, which was held in Salzburg, Austria. There, I had the opportunity to study with individuals from twelve countries from around the world. These and others were all very invaluable experiences.

After the completion of my fellowship, I was appointed as executive assistant to the president. The president immediately put me in charge of several projects. This was a great experience where I learned to deal with the challenges that presidents and other senior level administrators face on a daily basis. I later became the associate vice president for Academic and Student Affairs. In this position, I was responsible for the effective oversight of the entire Student Affairs division. My responsibilities included bridging the gap between academic affairs and student affairs, to increase the enrollment, and to enhance the retention and graduation rates. We were very successful in our efforts. Later, I was promoted to the executive vice president. In retrospect, upon my promotion to executive vice president, there were individuals who became envious of me, simply because of the positions that I held and because I was advancing very quickly. Later, President Spikes became very ill, and she could not come to campus. At this point, I was responsible for carrying out the wishes of the president while she was away. The president received notice from her doctor that her health was gradually getting worse. Therefore, she decided that it would be in her best interests to retire as president of UMES. This, unfortunately, is when I began to notice that specific administrators, alumni, and others were intentionally creating barriers to prevent me from becoming president of UMES. Although there were persons who did not want me to advance, I was later appointed as interim president by the University System of Maryland's Board of Regents. After this announcement, one Saturday morning, I woke up and noticed that there was an article on the front page of the newspaper stating that I was too young and had a quick temper, which was not true. The person quoted in the article disseminated fliers with negative things about me, my administration, and the recently retired president. I held my composure, however, and I refused to get involved in the negative politics that took place. I remained professional and focused on moving the university forward.

What Prompted Change To New Position

I was an applicant for the permanent presidency at UMES. However, there were individuals who worked diligently to ensure that the Board of Regents would not select me as the permanent candidate. Within eleven years of service at the university, I successfully navigated through the faculty and administrative ranks. I served in the following positions at UMES: professor of English, chair of the department of English and modern languages, executive assistant to the president, associate vice president for academic and student affairs and chief administrative officer of student affairs, executive vice president, and interim president. Ultimately, I was not successful in obtaining the permanent presidency as the internal candidate. Therefore, I returned to my first love, which was teaching, and I rejoined the faculty as a professor of English. I re-grouped and re-focused my career path and began to consider leadership opportunities at other institutions. It was quite exciting to be on the job market again after spending twelve years at one institution.

It was exciting because I knew that the sky was the limit to what I could do and where I could now go. It was as if someone had given me wings to fly again. I felt as though I had a clear mind to think big and to dream big again. I didn't know where I was going, but I knew that it was going to be great. After applying for various positions, I was fortunate to have been offered various kinds of interviews for senior-level administrative positions. It was refreshing to visit other institutions and examine how they were educating students, how they were addressing the new trends in higher education, how they were executing daily operations, how they were managing the finances, the academic enterprise, student affairs, and the University community.

I was selected for an interview for nearly every position for which I applied. Most of my interviews were at PWIs, and only a few interviews were at historically black colleges and universities (HBCU). Sometimes, I felt that I was just interviewed because I was the minority candidate in the pool. I was a finalist in several searches. I was told by several colleagues and mentors that it was going to be difficult to obtain a senior level position at a PWI because I had spent my career at HBCUs. However, I found this to be untrue. While this has been the traditional trajectory for some, I have been able to hold leadership positions at both PWIs and HBCUs. I believe that it is important for all institutions to have diversity at all levels of leadership. This is important because people from diverse backgrounds can bring their educational, cultural, social, and other experiences that can be shared and learned by others.

One of my mentors said, "We hope they will judge you on your merit and accomplishments because you have the necessary experience, knowledge, skills, and ability to obtain a senior-level position at an elite institution." I interviewed at an institution and was verbally offered a vice president's position by the president. I stated that I wanted to transfer my tenure and rank because I was already a tenured full professor. We kept negotiating for weeks. I thought we had settled the negotiations, and I was informed that I would receive a contract in the mail. I waited, and I waited. Weeks went by, and months went by, and I never received the contract that I was promised. I vowed that under my leadership incidents such as this would not occur.

In the meanwhile, I interviewed at Middle Tennessee State University (MTSU). After I returned home, a few days later the president called me and conducted a phone interview. He stated that I had really prepared myself for senior-level administration in higher education and he was impressed with my credentials. The president and the provost shared the campus evaluations from my interview with me. The responses were very positive, and the president stated, "We want you here at Middle Tennessee State University." I was hired at Middle Tennessee State University (MTSU) as the vice provost for academic affairs, a PWI that had nearly 23,000 students. Being at MTSU was a unique experience for me, particularly since I had spent my entire career at small HBCUs. I had now moved to a large PWI where I was among the minority rather than being among the majority at an HBCU.

I served as Interim Dean of the College of Continuing Education and Distance Learning while continuing to serve as vice provost for academic affairs. I was compensated for the extra duties that I performed as the interim dean. Eventually, I was promoted to senior vice provost for academic affairs. The Office of Cultural Diversity was now expanding into an Office of Institutional Diversity that consisted of all diversity components university-wide. I worked very closely with the president and the provost of the university, representing them both at meetings and at various functions both on campus as well as off campus. I continued to enjoy the work that I did as a senior-level administrator because I believed that I was making a difference in the lives of others. I chaired the graduation committee that was responsible for all commencement exercises. The most exciting part of the job and the most rewarding is when I see students going across the stage receiving their degrees. It is fulfilling because, as an administrator, I have played some role in helping the students achieve their goals whether directly or indirectly.

While I was at MTSU, the chair of the psychology department stated that there was a provost and academic vice president's position open at Western Illinois University (WIU). The chair of the department stated that I would be a good fit for the university and a good fit in working with the president of WIU. After many discussions, I decided to apply for the position. The interview, I believed, was one of the best that I had ever had. The people were genuinely friendly and showed a great deal of hospitality. They were concerned about the next person who would serve as their provost. I was offered the position of provost and academic vice president at WIU a few days later. It was a very difficult decision to accept the position especially because I had become immensely involved in the community. It was difficult to uproot my family and move to the Midwest, even though it was a move that would advance my career. I wanted to bring my family to Macomb, Illinois to see the university and the community.

After spending a couple of days in Macomb with my family, my wife and I decided that Western Illinois University was a place to begin the next chapter of my career. My wife would always say that she would support me in whatever decision I made about my career. She said I needed to be somewhere I was wanted. I have never heard her respond in such a way, so I knew it was the right decision and that Macomb, Illinois, was a place that we could call home.

Personal Leadership Experience

Serving in a senior level leadership position of an institution of higher education is a goal worth pursuing; however, this goal was partially achieved because of my involvement in various executive leadership programs including Kellogg NAFEO MSI Leadership Program, Harvard Leadership Program, Executive Leadership Summit, and the ACE Fellows Program. Through these initiatives, I along with countless other individuals have gained the self-confidence, mentoring, and experience that it takes to be leaders within the Academy. This is a highly competitive field and must be treated as such. The most qualified, skilled individual will undoubtedly have an edge on those who choose not to further their knowledge by taking advantage of these useful programs. Many of the programs differ in order to suit different individuals and their respective preferences.

The Kellogg NAFEO MSI Leadership Program was established to address the needs of minority serving institutions. The National Association for Equal Opportunity in Higher Education (NAFEO), which addresses the needs of African Americans, is part of the Kellogg MSI Leadership Fellow Program. The inaugural class began in 2003–2004 for three types of minority serving institutions: National Association for Equal Opportunity in Higher Education (NAFEO), American Indian Higher Education Consortium (AIHEC), and Hispanic Association of Colleges and Universities (HACU). The MSI Fellows Program was designed to prepare minorities for higher education administrative positions. Many of the presidents, particularly those who had retired, stated that they needed or wanted someone who was ready to step into the presidency and move the agenda forward. It was also stated that many individuals who had become new presidents did not have the preparation, knowledge, or experience to lead an HBCU. The Kellogg NAFEO Fellows Program was therefore created to prepare aspiring leaders for the trials they may face as a new president of an HBCU and address the overall needs of African Americans in leadership positions.

It is important to note that the individual workshops, seminars, and discussion groups focused on the specific type of university. For example, the NAFEO group dealt specifically with HBCU issues. This kind of approach is most beneficial to Fellows because minority-serving institutions have distinctive issues compared with PWIs, and even other colleges and universities when one considers cultural differences. The Kellogg NAFEO Fellows are enriched by university experiences that prepare them for the challenges that they face in HBCUs. They gain invaluable experience from listening and learning from current presidents as well as those who have retired. Of equal importance, the Fellows learn from leaders at public and private HBCUs. Experiences like these are important to enable individuals to lead various kinds of institutions and to ensure that administrators are prepared for such leadership.

I have spent the majority of my career at HBCUs; therefore, the Kellogg NAFEO Fellows Program was extremely helpful because it dealt specifically with issues that leaders face at black colleges and universities. Much of the discussion throughout the year-long experience (we met on designated dates during the academic year) centered upon the lack of resources, management, budget and finance, leadership skills, national trends, case studies, and "real-life experiences" from current and former presidents and other executive leaders. The generic sessions with NAFEO, AIHEC, and HACU Fellows enabled me to learn and have a more diverse experience. I held a full-time position while participating in the program, which made it difficult at times; however, spending a month at another HBCU was one of the most rewarding parts of the fellowship. I got a chance to focus full-time on my responsibilities as a fellow, shadow a president, work on a project at the visiting institution, and engage in the day-to-day activities of the office of the president. Because I was in the inaugural class for minority-serving institutions, our class set a precedent for future Fellows.

Like the NAFEO Fellows Program, the Executive Leadership Summit focused on HBCUs as well as national trends and other issues. This program differed strikingly from NAFEO's in that participants met for one intensive weekend (although I personally would like for it to be administered over a longer period of time) of activities that involved discussions and group participation. This specific program was established to address the issues of African American administrators. It began in 2001 at Hampton University. The program was primarily started by William Harvey—and became known as the "Harvey Executive Leadership Model–to train individuals for administrative positions. It is a two-day workshop that prepares individuals for many kinds of administrative experiences: "The Summit provides participants with an opportunity to receive professional development training from a cadre of highly successful executive leaders through stimulating lectures, case studies, interactive sessions and one-on-one dialogue" (*Chronicle of Higher Education,* Oct. 1, 2004, p. A51). The program is for "presidents (recently appointed), chancellors (recently appointed), provosts, assistant provosts, vice presidents, deans, assistant deans and other appointed executives" (*Chronicle of Higher Education,* Oct. 1, 2004, p. A51). The mission and vision of the summit is to:

1. Foster team-building and sharing of knowledge, skills, and abilities between those who hold executive positions and those who aspire to assume top leadership positions;
2. Create a network among those serving in the position of president at diverse small and mid-sized comprehensive universities and colleges with emphasis on the challenges presidents face in such settings;
3. Provide opportunities for aspiring executive officers to hear first-hand those challenges that presidents face as well as to be exposed to the range of strategies that current leaders have found successful;
4. Assist tomorrow's leaders in the development of strategies for accomplishing personal and professional goals;
5. Provide professional development and retooling for those who aspire to maintain excellence in their current leadership positions. (Hampton University Executive Leadership Summit, 2014)

I also served as an ACE Fellow. The ACE Fellows Program has been in existence since 1965 and is responsible for the training and leadership of hundreds of vice presidents, deans, chairs, faculty, and other emerging leaders. Through this unique program Fellows spend an extended period of time on another campus working directly with presidents. It condenses years of on-the-job experience and skills development into a single year (American Council on Education, 2014).

As an ACE Fellow, I had the opportunity to spend an entire year shadowing two presidents. Because I was on leave from my position, I was able to devote all of my time to being a fellow. I had the time to take in new knowledge and experiences, and to reflect upon and learn the new information. The invaluable experience helped me prepare to thrive in a life-long career in education administration. The ACE program afforded me the opportunity to gain knowledge and experiences regarding several kinds of institutions, which is very beneficial when seeking positions at colleges and universities of all sorts. The three leadership experiences afforded me the opportunity to become an agent for change. Networking was one of the most rewarding parts of all three programs. I made lifetime friends with whom I often speak informally when dealing with difficult issues and research opportunities. I certainly encourage other aspiring leaders to become involved in leadership programs as well.

CHAPTER 2

Academic Affairs and the University Presidency

The terms *university* and *college* have been long used interchangeably; however, there is a difference between the two entities. Universities typically provide instruction at the highest levels of learning, and this is why education at universities and other post–secondary levels is considered higher education. At its core, however, universities refer to the organizational structure of an institution. For example, universities are composed of academic colleges. Examples of the most common academic colleges in American universities are: Colleges of Arts and Sciences, Colleges of Business, Colleges of Education, Colleges of Music, and the like. Colleges are typically divided by academic disciplines. Further, colleges may be composed of various academic departments. Many American colleges have two or more academic departments. Although many colleges in the United States are constituent units of universities, there are many colleges that are independent of universities. These degree granting stand-alone colleges typically provide the same or similar educational programs and opportunities as universities. Thus, the primary difference between colleges and universities in the United States is their organizational, administrative, and/or governing structures.

It has been viewed that universities are more prestigious than colleges. However, that may not always be true. Although the trend has been for higher education entities to move toward using the term "university" some have continued to use college in their names. The College of William & Mary, Dartmouth College, Morehouse College, and Spelman College have not chosen to embrace the term "university" and are, arguably, no less prestigious than any university on titles alone. In Canada, a university is an educational institution that can grant degrees such as the bachelors, masters, and doctoral degrees, whereas colleges function more like community colleges in the United States and confer certificates or diplomas, but not degrees.

The University Presidency

I am a first-generation college student and a descendent of a working class family from the state of Alabama, and I am often asked, "What does a university president do?" In short, the duties of a university president consist of leading the entire university. A university president is the chief executive officer of the university. As the president of Western Illinois University, I serve as the chief executive officer and the primary spokesperson for the university. Western Illinois University is one university with two campuses; therefore, I provide overall leadership on both the Macomb and Quad Cities (Moline) campuses.

As president, I am primarily responsible for contributing to, communicating, and supporting the university's strategic vision and plan to ensure that the operational implementation of the strategic plan is successfully executed on each campus. I am also responsible for the implementation of all the board of trustees' policies and all other functions of the university. In partnership with the board of trustees, I am responsible for the fiscal stability of the university through wise management of revenue streams and the effective budgeting of university resources, from both public and private sources. As president, I manage a professional executive leadership team that includes vice presidents from academic affairs, student services, administrative services, advancement and public services, and Quad Cities and Planning. My presidential duties also include fostering the development, growth, involvement, and recognition of employees at all levels, empowering them by affirming that they are all valued members of the university community with important roles. In addition, as president, I am significantly involved in establishing and nurturing a collaborative campus culture that unites university stakeholders around the common purpose of the university's mission and goals. Finally, as president, I am well-positioned to provide leadership for the development and implementation of new programs, academic and otherwise.

A university president typically has earned a doctorate or holds an equivalent terminal professional degree. A university president often has substantial experience in higher education administration along with proven leadership, management, planning, fund-raising, public speaking, and organizational skills. There is not a clear path to the presidency. There has recently been a trend of university presidents being selected from outside of academia; however, these individuals, typically, have significant amounts of experience from within the private sector. University presidents have traditionally come from the academic side of the academy meaning those who have served as academic deans, academic vice presidents, and provosts. In recent trends, there have been a number of presidents coming from the student affairs side of university operations.

On a daily basis, a university president's job can be segmented into planning operations, internal relations and operations, and external relations and operations. There may be an imbalance of duties from day to day, but many of the duties overlap. As university president, one spends an enormous amount of time clarifying a vision, developing strategic plans, and implementing those plans using appropriate benchmarks. This is achieved through conducting a SWOT Analysis that analyzes a university's strengths, weaknesses, opportunities, and threats to determine the best course(s) of action and developing a good strategic plan.

Within clarifying a vision, a university may develop particular visions for the university including programs and facilities. The university president may spend portions of the work day developing and refining plans for appropriate construction projects or renovation of facilities. Vision may also include decision making with the executive team about opportunities to expand or adapt programs in student and community services. The university president also provides leadership supervision of the day–to-day operations of the university. On a daily basis, the university president must typically make many tough decisions related to budgetary matters, personnel matters, academic programs, community partnerships, and business partnerships. For example, as president, I meet often with the provost and academic vice president to discuss the hiring of senior level personnel, discussing academic programs including signature programs, deans, chairs and faculty. I often have meetings with community leaders, business and industry, the mayor, legislators and many others to discuss partnerships, opportunities of how we can work together, and ways in which we can enhance our professional relationships. I meet regularly with the budget director to create alternative scenarios and plans of action if there are budget reductions or cash flow problems. Of equal importance, we meet to discuss budget strategies and priorities.

Much of my time is spent with the president's executive leadership team (cabinet) for discussions, reflections, and feedback on major university issues and initiatives. Although there is an athletic director who is responsible for the oversight of the university's athletic programs, the university president is ultimately responsible for the successful implementation of and compliance with the rules of the National Collegiate Athletic Association (NCAA). The university president often hosts or travels to meet with national, regional, state, community, and business leaders and alumni associations. The university president is typically the individual who is most associated with the university from the perspective of the general public and the media. With few exceptions, the university president is the most visible person who represents the university. It is an expectation that university presidents sustain state funding while increasing private funding for the institution. The university president is responsible for identifying opportunities for the university to contribute socially, economically, and intellectually to the community, state, and region in which it is located.

It is a misnomer that the president is the head of the governing structure for the university. The board of trustees (or similar name), which is the governing body of most American institutions of higher education, has a board chairperson. This person is typically the head of the governing body for a university. In most cases, university presidents are hired by and held accountable by the university's board of trustees. The president reports to the university board of trustees, which is a group of individuals elected or selected by different constituencies including the governor and or state legislature (The board of trustees' major role is to establish the broad policy initiatives that guide the development of the university, but the day to day operations are the university president's responsibility). Communication is the key to a successful university presidency. The university president usually has a number of formal opportunities to communicate the vision for the university. Formal communication opportunities typically come through an annual state of the university address and other formal and informal speaking engagements.

Strategic Plans and Timetables

The strategic plan is a detailed document that communicates a university's mission, the university president's vision of the future, and the incremental steps that are needed to achieve its goals. A strategic plan normally takes six months to two years to plan and construct. This process may take longer if external forces cause some adjustments to be made. In developing a strategic plan, various constituencies are involved in the planning process. This includes administrators, faculty members, staffers, trustees, alumni, and even students. Outside consultants may also be hired by a university to engage in the planning process. The final document is usually submitted to the president and trustees or regents for approval. At Western Illinois University, the strategic plan is called *Higher Values in Higher Education*. The current plan has recently been updated to include new items in my presidential initiatives as well as general updates based on the economic trends that the university faces. The current strategic plan has been updated to extend to 2022. A major part of Western's strategic plan involves enrollment that has been a challenge for the university since the early 2000s. The university hired an enrollment consulting firm to help create an aggressive recruitment plan that focused on the demographics of the state of Illinois. The firm also focused on retention and graduation rates. The plan that was developed was implemented in an effort to sustain the student enrollment, retention, and graduation rates for a significant period of time in the future.

Strategic plans have become controversial, and some claim that strategic plans are irrelevant. In 2006, the chancellor of a large, public comprehensive university in the Midwest was forced to resign after it was discovered that much of its new strategic plan had been copied from a similar university. The chancellor had previously coordinated work on the strategic plan at another institution. In a similar vein, the president of a small private liberal arts college was forced to resign when it was noticed that his new plan seemed to have been copied from a much larger public institution. In instances like these, if plans are adopted from other institutions, then the appropriate citations should be included in the document.

Curriculum and Instruction

A curriculum is an organized body of information, principles, and theories comprising what a college or university teaches in courses (Cohen, 1998). The curriculum should be one of the most important concerns of the academic administration because it is (or should be) the primary focus of the mission of the university. University presidents may not focus on curricular matters as much as they should because presidents are usually concentrating on such other administrative matters as planning, fundraising, and building relationships. Provosts, deans, and chairpersons are usually more focused on curriculum and instructional matters. This includes meeting with curriculum committees and program reviewers, and engaging in conversations with faculty about courses and instructional pedagogy in the courses.

Knowledge is expanding so fast that new curriculums are being developed and universities are finding it difficult to keep pace. The expansion of scholarly information is creating opportunities for new major fields of study to be developed quickly; however, universities and university presidents must remain focused on their missions. Universities must identify what they do well. Based on this information, universities can remain focused on their strengths before expanding in a direction that may not meet the needs of their existing mission. Universities must use their strong and/or unique academic programs to their advantage. Well-known academic programs should be branded into signature programs. After signature programs have proven to be successful, I would advise that institutions begin to focus on identifying opportunities to expand in cutting edge areas that complement their current academic offerings. For example, a pharmacy program may prove to complement a successful nursing program. Curriculum development and expansion can derive from many sectors including student demand, accreditation agencies' demands, industry demands, and the societal needs. Students can pressure a change in the curriculum. If students do not take certain courses, after a number of academic years the courses should be removed from the academic catalog. Before these courses are removed from the curriculum, however, perhaps they should be repackaged and retooled. In some cases, courses have become obsolete. When I was an undergraduate at Alabama A&M University, students could enroll in a computer keyboarding course. With the advancement of computers and computer software since that time, however, today's student would not enroll in such a course, and it would be taken out of the academic catalog. In recent years, many individuals who are responsible for maintaining the curriculum for undergraduate and graduate academic programs have begun the practice of asking corporations, firms, and agencies to articulate the types of skills and knowledge that they expect their new hires to have. This practice, ideally, will help prepare a more qualified workforce and hiring pool from which companies can select college graduates for employment. This practice also allows faculty and academic administrators to strengthen the academic programs and relevance of these academic programs to societal needs and norms.

Even though the university president is removed from this process, he or she must be aware of the curricular trends because, ultimately, it is the president's responsibility to communicate changes and why some changes must or will occur. Changes to the curriculum may be conducted through self-study, ad hoc committees, external consultants, informed faculty, and product analyses. The university president and the leadership team must determine which method is the best for their particular university.

Construction, Facilities, Laboratories, and Library

Although a university president is concerned with the curriculum and instruction on the campus, a considerable amount of time is focused on construction and facilities. Planning for construction projects is a challenging activity, but it is fundamental to the university presidency because traditionally a president's success has been associated with campus expansion, program expansion, and fundraising regardless if there have been successes in other areas. In most states, the legislature has reduced allocations for constructing new facilities at public universities; therefore, public universities are encumbering increasing proportions of construction debt. When acquiring more debt, universities are risking their triple high grade bond ratings and facing even higher interest costs. The debt issue is causing some universities to postpone and/or cancel capital improvement and construction projects.

A general process for funding new construction projects at many state institutions involves university presidents and their leadership teams articulating an argument that supports the position that new facilities are needed. The university president must articulate a clear vision and purpose for the project and should be directly involved in persuading constituencies. Once gaining stakeholders and legislative support, the funding is usually provided by a state capital development entity. The next phase of the process includes university leadership collaborating with an architectural firm to develop plans for the structure. These plans and other descriptions of the facility are needed to create the bidding packet for state-approved contractors to bid on the project. The construction company that submits the lowest bid generally receives the contract.

A poorly executed facility renovation or poorly built new facility project may be counted as a blot on one's presidency. A university president must rely on the construction and contracting companies that secure the contract to control costs and ensure that projects are completed correctly and on time. In deciding whether to renovate a facility, it may be best not to renovate because of the rising costs that are associated with renovating facilities that are obsolete and may present a safety hazard. In this case, it may be best to demolish it. An example of such a case is the implosion of Wetzel Hall, which was a high-rise residence hall that was built in the 1960s at Western Illinois University. Over the years the residence hall had become a safety hazard. A study of the building revealed that it would require significant renovations to be brought up to modern standards. As a result, it was imploded. In essence, tough decisions have to be made for the betterment of the university. The university president must make sure that the companies have a good construction plan because this is the basis for developing the budget and the schedule for work, and overages in either area can be costly to the university. University presidents are often placed under pressure to handle unexpected emergency situations. For example, in the summer of 2012, there was a fire and a flood in Currens Hall, which is an academic building that houses many science laboratories on the campus of Western Illinois University. As president, I was well positioned to respond to the occurrence immediately.

Although some of the factors that contribute to a successful presidency have changed over the years, presidential leaders must remain vigilant, think ahead, and consider the big picture. At one time, the size and the number of books physically available in the university's library was a part of the formula for a president's success. Since the advent of online journals, periodicals, books, and others electronic materials, the success of the library is no longer measured by traditional indicators. Although libraries have evolved, university presidents must still work with the library leadership to ensure that this facility remains a focal point of the university. Further, the library must continue to provide programming and instructional services that help to enhance the overall academic experience on campus. Traditionally, libraries have been academic havens on campuses where students, faculty, staff, and external constituents (primarily the community) can gather for intellectual inquiry and programming.

A university president and the director of the physical plant (or facilities management on some campuses) should develop a prioritized list of projects. This list should be reviewed and revised periodically and shared with the campus community. This project list outlines the campus priorities and is a direct indicator that the university president is aware and involved in the maintenance of university grounds and facilities.

Undergraduate Programs

According to Thelin (2011), the colonists created institutions for higher education for several reasons. New England settlers included many alumni of the royally chartered British universities, Cambridge and Oxford, and therefore believed education was essential (Thelin, 2011). In addition, the Puritans emphasized a learned clergy and an educated civil leadership. Their outlook generated Harvard College in 1636. Between Harvard's founding and the start of the American Revolution, the colonists chartered nine colleges and seminaries, although only one in the South. Religion provided an impetus for the creation of colonial colleges (Thelin, 2011).

Colonial colleges were small in size and limited in scope, and they rarely enrolled more than one hundred students, few of whom completed their degrees (Thelin, 2011); however, the young men who attended these colonial colleges made historic and extraordinary contributions to both political thought and action. Colleges also represented one of the few institutional ventures to receive royal and/or colonial government support and regulation during the eighteenth century (Thelin, 2011). The college's multipurpose buildings were typically among the largest construction projects in the colony, and they were matched only by a major church or a capitol. With the founding of the United States, governmental policies toward English-chartered colleges became unclear (Thelin, 2011). Wary of centralized power, Americans maintained educational control close to home. Governance of colonial colleges therefore became almost exclusively the jurisdiction of local and state governments. In actuality, the schools enjoyed independence as the Supreme Court's famous *Dartmouth* decision in 1819 demonstrated that the new federal government would protect colleges from state intervention (Thelin, 2011).

With the reputation of colleges remaining high, most state legislatures, particularly in the newer states west of the Allegheny and Appalachian mountain ranges, looked favorably on chartering colleges as long as the state did not have to provide financial support (Thelin, 2011). Between 1800 and 1850, the United States experienced a "college building boom" in which more than two hundred degree-granting institutions were created; however, because most of these new colleges depended on student tuition payments and local donors, there was also a high closure rate, and the schools that did survive typically struggled from year to year. Going to college early in the nineteenth century was not particularly expensive. The cost of potential lost opportunities presented a greater concern for students and parents. Employers seldom required college degrees; therefore, college presidents faced the perpetual challenge of persuading young adults to delay pursuing their life's enterprises by spending four years on campus. Modest-income families decided whether or not a young man's potential contribution to family labor could be spared while he pursued higher education. Although the classical languages and liberal studies of the bachelor of arts degree remained central to the character of American higher education in this era, several new fields gained a foothold in formal study (Thelin, 2011).

Graduate Programs

In 1861, Yale University was the first school to offer doctorates. By 1900 doctorates had become a staple in higher education (Yale University website, 2013). To obtain a master's degree, one must have acquired a bachelor's degree. With regard to graduate schools, there is a distinction between graduate schools and professional schools. Professional schools usually offer specialized degrees in medicine, law, or business. Graduate school is more like an apprenticeship. Instead of taking structured courses for few hours, graduate school is more time consuming because it is usually more research based.

In deciding whether to establish new graduate programs, the university president and the leadership team must determine if the university possesses the financial and physical resources to expand graduate programs. It must also be determined what graduate programs will be expanded at the university. High-demand graduate programs are typically good for universities, but depending on university's resources moderately competitive programs may also be a good fit. Graduate programs can be centralized and operated by a graduate dean or graduate director, or they can be decentralized and operated by academic deans of individual colleges. Universities usually have graduate faculty status that is based on criteria set by the university, but it usually means that a person is qualified and has been trained to teach and conduct research with graduate students. This designation also means that the faculty member has an established publishing record and is usually ranked as an associate or full professor.

Many graduate programs provide financial support through an assistantship or fellowship; however, these assistantships or fellowships are, usually, highly competitive and, typically, reserved for high-achieving students. Assistantships and fellowships usually cover tuition and fees, and, in many cases, a stipend is also provided to the student to cover living expenses. Often, assistantships are for teaching and research, and students are required to teach undergraduate courses and or assist a professor in conducting research. Students who receive fellowships or assistantships are more likely to accept an admissions offer from a university. Universities that wish to build strong graduate programs must find ways to help fund students. This funding should be built into the university's academic budget. Successful graduate programs should also grant supplemental funding to graduate students who chose to come to their universities. When I arrived at Western Illinois University as provost and academic vice president, I implemented the requirements for a feasibility study for new programs. Feasibility studies are necessary to ensure that there is enough funding, students, and course offerings for programs to grow over time.

Distance Learning and Online Programs

Distance learning and online programs and the use of technology have become a common instructional medium in the new era of higher education. In fact, the underpinning of distance education can be traced back to the use of correspondence courses. The use of technology in the classroom can be traced back to Patrick Suppes and Richard Atkinson, Stanford University psychology professors who used computers to teach math computations to elementary school students during the 1960s (Atkinson, 1968). In 1963, Bernard Luskin installed the first computer in a community college for instruction, and while working with Stanford and others, developed computer assisted instruction (Ionescu, 2012). Luskin completed his landmark UCLA dissertation working with the Rand Corporation in analyzing impediments to computer-assisted instruction in 1970 (Ionescu, 2012). As early as 1993, William D. Graziadei described an online computer-delivered lecture, tutorial and assessment project using electronic mail. By 1994, the first online high school had been founded (Ionescu, 2012).

Distance learning and on-line education can be a new frontier for universities. With the trend of spiraling student enrollment, for many university presidents, distance learning and on-line programs have been a means of maintaining student growth by expanding educational opportunities to individuals who may not be able to attend classes in a traditional face-to- face course model. Although not widely publicized, many elite universities have added on-line course offerings and offer on-line degrees. There are advantages and disadvantages to distance learning and on-line programs. Distance learning and online programs allow students to earn their education around their schedules. In these difficult economic times, students are arguably forced to work and work more hours while pursuing their degree. Distance learning allows students to meet their financial challenges while taking courses.

Online and distance learning programs allow nontraditional students who hold full time employment who might want to pursue graduate studies to also enroll in courses. For universities in rural regions, this allows students who are not within reasonable commuting distance to enroll in courses and possibly build relationships with entities in the students' home community. Online education can allow brick and mortar universities to expand beyond our boundaries. Our brick and mortar universities have limited space to be utilized and the number of students who can be admitted. Universities have limitations, and in many cases distance learning and on-line programs will allow the university to go beyond these limitations. As universities strive to become more military friendly, these types of programs are instrumental for military personnel who are fulfilling their military obligations while still pursuing higher education. This also means that distance learning and on-line degree programs will continue to provide access to students and boost student enrollments.

There has been criticism of distance learning and online programs. These programs call for an updated technology infrastructure at the university. The internet is a key vehicle in course delivery of online courses. It is therefore essential that adequate internet connection is available. Students and faculty will become frustrated if the connection and transmission are inadequate. Some distance-learning programs use "synchronous" technology to allow all partici-pants to be active at the same time. If streaming technology is being used to watch faculty lectures, frustration can set in if technology needs do not meet student needs. "Asynchronous" technology allows students to participate at different times. With both synchronous and asynchronous technology, universities are required to have adequate internet connections that respond quickly and can meet the needs of the students and faculty, and this has been a problem for some universities.

Some online programs have been criticized for an alleged lack of rigor. Critics claim that students do not learn as much online as they can learn in a face-to-face course. Another criticism of online education, specifically for-profit colleges, is the perception of poor quality of instruction and a continual enrollment of students without any concern for their learning and outcomes. If this is the case, perhaps accrediting agencies could provide more oversight for universities who offer on-line courses. This oversight may help ease the concerns of students and other stakeholders. Critics also state that on-line programs breed isolation and a disconnection from universities. They believe that being at a college and soaking up the atmosphere is a part of the learning experience (Tucker, 2001).

This criticism can be combatted by establishing an oversight office to monitor the quality of distance and online programs. These courses should undergo the same kinds of curriculum review as traditional face-to-face courses. Training in course development must be the central purpose for the operations that will oversee the management of distance and on-line programs. Some faculty will be resistant to moving some courses to an online format. The university president, however, must convince key stakeholders that education is changing and those who do not change will be at a disadvantage as the technology and the method in which a college education is delivered moves forward.

CHAPTER 3

The Community and the University Presidency

Universities and their surrounding communities historically have had tumultu-
ous relationships in regards to working to address common problems. The mission of universities should serve a cause larger than themselves. As far back as
the late 1880s, there have been tensions between the universities and their surrounding communities (Thelin, 2011). In 1889, the University of Chicago opened
'Hull House,' which was a university–community partnership created to help the
low-income families of Chicago's west side adjust to the proliferation of urbanization and industrialization (Lissak, 1989).

In the United States, hostility toward universities was initially developed
because universities were built in inaccessible areas away from communities.
Universities were often located in rural and remote areas far removed from the
economic and social problems of the broader society and surrounding community. Out of this, universities promoted themselves as elite bastions of information and knowledge, and, quite frankly, university personnel erroneously
thought that they were better than those persons who were not associated with
the university. Professors and students attired in their academic gowns were
as distinct from townsfolk as university campuses were from their surrounding architectures. This separation is captured in the often invoked expression,
"town and gown," which also captures the tension between the two. This tension was famously captured in Spike Lee's movie, *School Daze*, between the
students from fictional Mission College and the "local townspeople." A pivotal
scene in that movie, one of the local men tells the students, "Ya'll (college students) ain't no better than us."

Despite their beginnings in isolated places, universities were engulfed in
their expanding surrounding communities. Many universities were simply over-
whelmed by their surrounding communities as these communities began to see
the economic advantages of having college students spend money in town, and
they began to establish more businesses. The response of many universities to en-
croaching urbanization was to build higher walls and stronger gates in an attempt
to maintain a separation from their surrounding communities. In response, many

colleges choose to remain disconnected from their surrounding community. Out of this, colleges grew more self-centered and focused on problems within the academy and not on the complex problems of the larger society.

Fundraising Campaigns

Fundraising is the heartbeat of a university presidency. According to the Council for Aid to Education Voluntary Support of Education Survey, contributions to the nation's colleges and universities received $30.30 billion in charitable contributions to colleges and universities in the United States in 2011 (Council for Aid to Education, 2012). The largest source of donations to universities and colleges come from foundations; the second largest source comes from alumni; and the third largest source comes from corporations. There are several factors to be considered when launching a long-term capital project, endowment campaign, or annual campaign. To be successful at any of these campaigns, a university president should build a good fundraising team and create a positive relationship between staff and volunteers. Recruiting and retaining volunteers are essential to assist with making a university's fundraising campaign successful. Successful fundraising can enhance a university's public image and provide essential dollars to the coffers of the university (Council for Aid to Education, 2012).

A university president spends enormous amounts of time fundraising. In doing so, one must be keenly aware and gain a good understanding of the processes of fundraising. A university president must understand that fundraising is not a one-time occurrence. Fundraising is a perpetual process, but donors should never feel as if you are constantly asking them for their money. A university president must let the university's values guide the process and appeal to donors and convince them that they are giving to a worthwhile cause. Good stewardship of all funds received from donors is essential to building great donor relationships and obtaining future financial contributions. University presidents and their fundraising staffs must build a case and educate the public on what is special and distinctive about their university. Because of magnificent branding and long histories of wealthy alumni, it is easy for Stanford University and Harvard University to solicit funds and have multimillion dollar fundraising campaigns. It is easy for flagship state-supported universities through their signature and high-profile academic and sports programs to have successful multimillion dollar campaigns.

These two types of universities utilize their uniqueness to appeal to donors. Every university has something special about it. It is the responsibility of the university president to assemble a team to determine how the institution should articulate uniqueness. Yale University and Columbia University can make unique cases of appeals for funding, but historically black institutions, like Howard University and Hampton University, have unique cases as well. For example, Claflin University in Orangeburg, South Carolina, has embarked on its "Campaign for Claflin" where its goal is to raise $96.4 million (Claflin, 2011). Claflin's appeal is easily found on the front of its university's webpage. Claflin University states the following in its mission statement:

> The Campaign for Claflin University is designed to enhance the University's emerging profile as one of the premier undergraduate teaching and research universities in the world. The campaign focuses on three priorities for Claflin; devoting $13.9 million to strengthen academic programs; $41 million to enhance the university's infrastructure, including the construction of a new state-of-the-art science and technology center; and $41.5 million to build an endowment which will provide scholarships and financial aid to promising students and aid in the recruitment of top ranked faculty.

Claflin's request statement for funds is clear and transparent about how the funds collected will be used. Openness is essential because donors want to know how their contributions are going to be used. Fundraising is a voluntary exchange in which presidents must take the lead and persuade people to give, but again potential donors should not feel pressured, quilted, or intimidated into giving. Ethical behavior is required in being successful in fundraising. It is also important that donors be kept abreast of the status of the fundraising campaign. Claflin does that by providing a report on their website. In August 2012, the website indicated that:

> To date, supporters have already committed nearly $58 million towards the campaign goal. A large portion of those contributors include members of the university community, corporate and business partners, churches, local government, and alumni and friends.

Giving to a university is an honor and a privilege and not a burdensome albatross. University presidents must convince past and potential donors that they want to be a part of something great and larger than themselves. Fundraising has become more difficult since the downturn in the economy in 2007 and the trend of state and federal government reducing appropriations to public colleges and universities. University presidents must continue to appeal to potential donors' sense of purpose and goodness. Presidents must appeal to donors' humanity and sell the social benefit of donating to their university. Universities must produce successful results. Everyone typically wants to be affiliated with a high-quality organization or association. When a university produces positive results, whether they are academic or athletic results, people want to be a part of this success and presidents must harness this enthusiasm and encourage people to give.

Top Fundraising Universities in the United States 2012	
Stanford University	$1.035 billion
Harvard University	$650 million
Yale University	$544 million
University of California Los Angeles	$492 million
Columbia University	$490 million
Johns Hopkins University	$480 million
University of Pennsylvania	$441 million
University of California Berkeley	$405 million
New York University	$396 million
University of Southern California	$379 million
University of Texas at Austin	$354.34 million
Duke University	$349.66 million
New York University	$337.85 million
Washington University	$334.49 million
University of Wisconsin Madison	$315.77 million
Cornell University	$315.53 million

Source: The Chronicle of Higher Education

University presidents should be familiar with the fundraising cycle. Fundraising is a conscience well-designed process. Fundraising in universities has long been a part of the landscape of higher education. The first step in fundraising for university presidents is to lead their team in analyzing the needs of the university. These requirements can be determined through needs assessment planning. This requires an honest assessment by those who are familiar with and are invested in the university and the president's vision for the university. When goals and priorities are set, then preparations for fundraising are set to begin.

The needs assessment equips the university president's team with the necessary tools to develop a formal statement of needs and appeal document. This statement should be vetted by various stakeholders who are invested in the university. Volunteers can be essential in this process because many will come from outside the silos of academe and provide a fresh perspective in refining the final appeal. A poorly developed needs statement can be the difference between a successful and an unsuccessful fundraising campaign.

Once the needs statement has been created, the university must define the goals and objectives of the campaign. The objectives provide specific explanations of how a particular goal will be accomplished. In creating these goals, the team must establish a link to the university and provide a well-defined rationale for the donors to give. A realistic fundraising goal should be sought and then a figure immediately beyond that figure should be the goal of the campaign. A realistic timeframe for the campaign should be set. It is unrealistic to think that a university can embark on a successful fundraising campaign to raise $60 million over a twelve - to eighteen-month period. This may prove difficult even for the elite universities in the United States. One must be realistic in setting the timeframe. My predecessor at Western Illinois University, President Alvin Goldfarb, set the university on a path to raise $60 million over a five-year period. After President Goldfarb retired in 2011, I was selected as president of Western Illinois University. I was committed to continue the campaign and reach the $60 million goal. In 2013, WIU reached its campaign goal.

Once the needs statement has been prepared and financial goal has been set, effective management of the fundraising process is essential. This process must follow sound practices of project management, determine the goal, develop a plan, implement the plan, and evaluate the plan. One of the most important, if not the most important factors in launching and having a successful fundraising campaign, is communicating the case for financial support. This begins with the university president. The university president must be able to communicate in a compelling manner why individuals should give to their university. This takes talent and skill and should be honed before making appeals for donations. This calls for creativity in communicating one's case. In today's technological environment, universities should master such social media technologies as Facebook and Twitter, among others. Fundraising through technology was first introduced with Howard Dean's presidential campaign in 2004, and President Barack Obama made fundraising through technology commonplace. University presidents can engage students and young alumni by using technology. Once the appeal for funds has been articulated within the university and in the community, volunteers will be needed to assist in soliciting potential donors.

Fundraising should be a campus-wide initiative, where faculty, staff, administrators, and students should all establish fundraising goals to ensure that the university meets its mark. The university president must cultivate a culture of fundraising where all see themselves as fundraisers for the university. Each of the individuals represents a growing force and advocates for the university. All of the previous preparation leads to the next and most important part of fundraising—asking for money. In asking, it is important to let the potential donor know what their investment will do and appeal to the humanity in the individual. The perspective donors must know that their donations will allow the institution to improve the lives of the students enrolled at the university. Asking and then receiving the donation is often considered the ending task but it is actually the beginning. It is beginning because it is hoped that it is the start of a relationship where the donor will make contributions year after year. The university must practice sound business and accounting practices including disclosure when handling donations from the public. A university must continually evaluate its fundraising processes to make them efficient. Then fundraising efforts may be tweaked and or expanded in response to the evaluation.

Presidential Transition

My transition to the presidency was most unique as compared with many other university presidents. I was an internal candidate who had served as provost and academic vice president under my predecessor's leadership. The former president, Al Goldfarb, had four months remaining on his contract before I officially took the helm of the university. During the four-month transitional period, President Goldfarb and I conferred on various issues to ensure that the transition from his tenure to mine would be seamless in the operation of the university. Also during this period, Al Goldfarb was able to complete projects that were crucial to his presidency, and I was able to begin projects that would help to shape my vision—which would be a campus-wide shared vision. This transition period allowed me to introduce my leadership style to both campuses while setting the priorities for the university, and introducing my future plans for the university. I recommend, if possible, that more universities utilize this transitional model because it provides institutional leaders an opportunity to discuss institutional culture, history, traditions, and climate. In addition, I was able to discuss all of the facets of the institution with my predecessor, including budgetary matters, political issues, personnel matters, and other past, current, and future issues. The transitional period and the first year of the presidency is a time that many call the "honeymoon" period. During this period, many people tend to gravitate and seek leadership from the president. This is a very crucial time during the presidency because actions during this period will set the tone for the university.

Public Relations and the University Presidency

The role of university president and the university's public relations' team should provide a seamless and coordinated effort of community outreach. This community outreach should foster strong relationships with internal and external stakeholders to enhance support for the university. The public relations' team should assist and should work in concert with the president and all of the internal and external stakeholders of the university to garner the support necessary to fulfill the university's mission and accomplish its strategic goals. In doing so, the public relations' team at a university should be instrumental in assisting the president in implementing and communicating the vision for fundraising, marketing, alumni relations, and government relations. The public relations' team should be essential in building successful collaboration with partners in its immediate community and beyond. The efforts of the public relations' team should be progressive and include an integrated program that will galvanize people and inspire philanthropic giving of students, parents, alumni, faculty and staff, corporations, foundations, and friends of the university.

The university public relations department should be committed to informing the public and the university community about the quality and diversity of the learning environment at the university and the level of teaching, scholarship, research, and service. The university must keep the community informed of activities taking place on the campus and, whenever possible, the university should assist the community in finding practical solutions to community issues. The public relation's team must help the president manage the message of the university by maintaining the excellence of core communications capabilities, including video, web, and social media, and build a support communications strategy.

With the growth of social media, it is difficult to manage all communication. An instance where the message could not be managed was the sexual misconduct at Penn State University. The scandal caused by this issue became international. Penn State University leaders allegedly did not report incidents of sexual misconduct on the part of an individual who was employed as an assistant football coach. The way the leadership team, including the university president, handled the situation was reprehensible. The reverence for football at the university allowed these university officials to turn a blind eye to the allegations that had taken place over fifteen years. Justice was served as the perpetrator was convicted of forty-five counts of child molestation. The board of trustees commissioned Louis J. Freeh, a former FBI director, to investigate how the university handled this situation. Freeh and his team interviewed some 400 people and reviewed close to 3 million documents and produced a 267-page report that condemned the response of university leaders' handling of the scandal and the cover-up. Penn State University officials were apparently unfamiliar with the Clery Act. The *Jeanne Clery Disclosure of Campus Security Policy and Campus Crime Statistics Act (Clery Act)* is a federal mandate requiring all colleges and universities that participate in the federal student financial aid program to disclose information about crime on their campuses and in the surrounding communities. The *Clery Act* affects virtually all public and private universities. The Clery Act is enforced by the U.S. Department of Education.

The university was ultimately held liable. The NCAA has created a task force to assist Penn State in managing the $60 million fine handed down after the child molestation scandal. The money will fund programs designed to combat child sexual abuse and help victims throughout the country. The task force will set policy and hire a third-party administrator who will choose which non-profit groups receive the funds each year. The NCAA imposed tough sanctions on Penn State over its handling of sex-abuse allegations against a retired assistant football coach convicted of abusing ten boys. The governing body acted swiftly following a school-sanctioned report. Some school officials have vehemently denied Freeh's allegations in the report. The university was also penalized by the NCAA. The NCAA levied a four-year postseason ban, significant scholarship cuts, and other sanctions. University presidents must protect the brand and image of the university, but this should never be above doing the right thing. The right thing for Penn State was to turn the child predator in to the authorities and let justice be served through the legal system.

In Illinois, the Illinois Department of Children & Family Services requires each university employee to report child abuse whenever there is a reasonable cause to believe that a known child is being abused or neglected. A hotline number is also provided to take calls of alleged abuse. This measure assists in curtailing these kinds of crimes on campuses, but university employees must also report these kinds of incidences. The university's culture should promote high performance and ethical behavior as a part of this culture. The university president's leadership team should also assist the president in promoting a culture of high performance and provide policies for managing communication for the entire university. Community relations should be central to the university's message. The university must be involved in the community by serving on boards of community based organizations and local business associations. Communication and community relations should never be above doing the right thing.

University President and State and Local Governments

In the United States, most universities were founded and are operated by state government. The University of North Carolina and the University of Georgia are the oldest designated public institutions (Thelin, 2011). Although the College of William & Mary was founded earlier, it was first designated as a private college (Thelin, 2011). Each state in the United States operates at least one public university. In building relations with public officials, they should be reminded of the economic impact that the university and its students, faculty, and staff have on their local economy. Within this report, they should be reminded specifically how many people the university employs and the amount of tax revenue that is generated by the university. If this is not being done, then the university is missing a grand opportunity to communicate its significance to the local community. The university should develop and maintain relationships with local elected officials and their staffs and municipal departments. The university president should develop good relationships with the city's mayor and the members of the city council. These relationships are important to growth and success of the university and its initiatives. Whenever possible, university presidents or their designee should invite elected officials to campus as speakers and guests at special events. The university should host educational forums on critical community issues, and more importantly do everything possible to make visitors feel comfortable while on campus. Many of them have not stepped foot on a college campus. If their experience is not a good one, many will not return to campus and they will not make any kind of contributions to the university, nor support its efforts. Universities and university presidents are being burdened by outdated technology, crumbling buildings on campuses, capital projects, and high-stakes competition for students. State and local governments are going to fund the construction they need, either through appropriations or by issuing their own debt. Public colleges and universities are likely to issue their own debt to finance the renovation of their facilities. By financing their own debt, public universities are moving closer to the practices of private universities. With the recent difficult economic times, more cost has been passed on to the students in the form of higher tuition and fees.

In 2012, the state of Illinois owed Western Illinois University $12.5 million from the previous fiscal year. This was complicated by a crisis in the state retirement system, which led to a high rate of retirements in 2012. This wave of retirements allowed for the university to continue to hire new faculty and avoid layoffs and furloughs. The decision was made to utilize funds from the university reserves until the financial challenges subside. If these trends continue, it will have a negative impact on the university's bottom line, and we will have to reprioritize our capital projects, and hold back on campus goals and initiatives, and identify new funding sources and revenue streams.

For universities to remain financially successful, institutional revenues must keep pace with the amount of debt that is assumed. Since 1999, a public university in the Midwest borrowed $626 million to build twenty-one new buildings (Kiley, 2012). The borrowing for this capital growth was to meet a projected student body growth and student demand. This put this institution at its debt limit. Just as in personal debt, taking on enormous debt can lower the university's credit rating and hamper its ability to borrow money in emergencies. This institution's plight is becoming the story for many universities. Universities are borrowing to build new buildings while the upkeep of the buildings on the existing campus is deteriorating. The state cannot bail them out, and the longer maintenance gets deferred the more expensive it will cost to repair these buildings in the future. Buildings that are in need of repairs are sometimes causing prospective students to choose other schools, resulting in decreased tuition revenue and fees, and less money for building and campus maintenance. Campuses that identify the problem early and develop a comprehensive plan for facility renewal are the ones that will survive and prosper.

It appears that this is the new normal for universities, and institutions should begin searching for new financial streams of revenue. The outlook for universities may be bleak with small numbers of traditional college-age students, aging campuses, less capital, more borrowing, and colleges approaching their debt limits. This may lead to colleges and universities tapping into resources allocated for other priorities, such as faculty salaries and student services. States and local governments that have traditionally issued bonds for institutions are facing a public crisis that is increasingly critical of government debt and higher taxes.

University and the Federal Government

Universities and the federal government have been partners in higher education. As a result of the 1862 Morrill Act, the federal government gave each eligible state 30,000 acres of federal land to sell to finance public institutions offering courses of study in such practical fields as agricultural and industrial studies, as well as liberal arts (Thelin, 2011). The state and federal governments play an important role in the advancement of universities. There are two key reasons why the federal government invests in higher education. The federal government supports activities within higher education where it believes there is a primary federal responsibility. A university's research can advance a compelling interest of the federal government. The federal government and higher education institutions have partnered to sustain basic and applied research that is in the national interest. One clear example would be technology and weaponry for the military. Federal support comes in a number of ways but mainly through funding, regulation of federally funded activities, and mandates to the states and universities to pursue areas of national interests. Universities receive money from federal work-study programs and federal student loans and grants. Although this money is given to students, it is ultimately supposed to be used for students to pay tuition and other fees in pursuit of their education. The federal government also provides federal money for research. This research support comes through many federal sources. The National Science Foundation, the Institute of Medicine, the Department of Energy, and the Department of Defense are examples of federal funding agencies that provide money for research as a compelling interest of the federal government.

Alumni Relations and the University President

The university president should maintain good relations with the university's alumni. It is paramount to make recurrent efforts to reach out to alumni, and communication efforts are a part of this relationship. A well-informed alumni base is more likely to support the university's efforts with positive public relations, volunteer time, and philanthropy. One vehicle that universities have much success in is informing alumni through alumni magazines. The alumni magazine should be an upscale glossy magazine with a number of photo images. Whenever possible, articles on successful faculty, students, and alumni should be prominently featured in this publication. This magazine can keep alumni informed of campus happenings and build better substantive connections to their university. There should be at least two issues per year distributed to the alumni, and these magazines should be mailed first class. The extra postage is worth the benefits of staying in touch and having mail forwarded. These magazines also should be distributed to potential donors as well as to governmental officials. The university should also consider including "change-of-address" forms in alumni magazines that can be completed and returned. These are sometimes passed on to other alumni who want to be on the mailing list. The alumni magazine should also have an electronic version and list serves for younger, more electronic-savvy alumni. With some alumni associations, Facebook is replacing the traditional alumni magazine. In 2010, the Council for Advancement and Support of Education conducted a national survey of alumni magazine readers (Jaschik, 2010). The results showed alumni magazines still held loyal readers who used the magazines to keep up with classmates and connect to their alma mater. The survey also suggests that alumni magazines are much less popular with younger alumni.

The university president and the alumni office should always have additional alumni magazines available to disseminate to those who may be interested. The alumni magazine can be used as a calling card to initiate new relationships and to develop existing ones. Some exemplary alumni magazines include University of Minnesota's *Minnesota Magazine*, Penn State's the *Penn Stater*, Carleton College's the *Voice*, and the Fashion Institute's the *Hue*. A smaller university that does an excellent job of producing its alumni magazine is Alabama State University, a historically black university located in Montgomery, Alabama. The *ASU Today Magazine* has been distributed to alumni for almost thirty years. It possesses featured stories of successful alumni, current students, and faculty. The operation of this alumni magazine requires that the university keep updated records of names, addresses, and its alumni.

The university must also invite the alumni back to campus periodically. This provides alumni from different eras to build relationships. This can create a synergy that may generate fond memories of the university that may lead them to give to the university. On and off campus special events for alumni and friends allow various constituencies to pursue an interest or connect with a specific group. Homecoming has traditionally been the time that alumni have decided to return for a visit to the university. The university's alumni office should oversee the day–to-day relations with alumni and encourage them to get involved or maintain involvement with the university. An alumni council or association can assist in building a higher level of understanding, insight, and knowledge of the university's commitment to being a learning community, being financially strong, and focusing its mission. Alumni can assist with student orientation, commencement ceremonies, career development, and hosting and attending events. The alumni director and alumni relations staff should follow up on any inquiry from alumni. The university president should be central to any efforts that are made by the alumni relations office.

Budgeting and the University Presidency

University budgeting and financial management involve the allocation of resources. Typically, these resources are provided to all units within the university. In Illinois, similar to most states, the fiscal year begins July 1 and ends June 30. Some states actually have a two-year—long fiscal year. A budget sheet discloses the priorities of organizations. Those things that are important to a unit usually receive adequate resources, and these are indicated on a budget sheet. The budgeting process also pertains to purchasing goods and services, and managing debt wisely. A university president must be able to manage financial resources effectively. A university budget illustrates the directions and goals of a university. The budget and the budgeting process allow the university to manage money and other resources that include allocations from the state, student tuition, student fees, and gifts and other contributions. Tuition is only a portion of the revenue that a university receives. Most states appropriate funding to universities each year. A state's revenue is largely based on the taxes that it receives each year. In years of financial growth, universities usually do not have to concern themselves with reduced allocations from the state; however, in challenging economic times, states may ask universities to make budget cuts and to reduce allocations to universities. Each year the university administration and other units determine the budget priorities and what should be included in operating and capital budgets presented to the state legislature. The administration reviews the budget submissions and compiles the information into a single report before forwarding the request to the state legislature. The budget and supporting documents are then submitted to the Illinois Board of Higher Education.

The Illinois Board of Higher Education compiles a report of recommendations (budget requests). After discussions with various sectors of higher education, the recommendation is then forwarded to the governor and the state legislature. The governor then submits the budget to the general assembly. The general assembly, which includes both chambers, reviews the requests and makes recommendations in the appropriation hearings. Universities are expected to send representatives to the appropriation committee meeting to clarify their funding request if needed. The legislature acts on the appropriation bill (both capital and operating). Once the general assembly approves and passes the budget, the budget is then sent to the governor. The governor has sixty days to act on the appropriations. The governor has line item authority and therefore can make changes to the budget. Once the new fiscal year begins, there is a sixty-day lapse period to complete all previous and pending transactions. After the lapse period, the new appropriations are dispersed. The board approves the budget summary for operations for the fiscal year. The state legislature meets to review the governor's actions on appropriations. Capital budgets and debt management are two key components in the fiscal management of universities. A capital budget is usually a part of a long-term planning process and a part of a capital investment plan where a timetable for various projects is set, along with schedules for their completions and the method of their financing. This investing plan usually covers a three to five year period and this plan is progressed forward each fiscal year.

The university administration must invest in the university's infrastructure, facilities, and equipment. Most universities have separate capital budgeting that manages most expenditures. Capital budgets also force most universities to think long term, which is sometimes a different philosophy from that which prevails in the regular budgeting process. A capital budget, however, can become a method of avoiding fiscal responsiveness and responsibility by some presidents. Some universities try to raise money for capital projects and not borrow money for their projects during the fiscal year in which they are authorized; however, most universities borrow money for large capital projects. Borrowing money can also be used for several reasons, but the university's bond rating is very important. A university's bond rating is like a person's credit score. The better the FICA score, the lower the interest rate that one qualifies. Likewise, the better the university's bond rating the lower the interest rate the university pays on the borrowed money. Standard and Poor's reference guides the rate bonds in descending quality from AAA to AA to A to BBB to BB and so on. Triple A, is the best and should be the gold standard for all universities. High ratings allow for bonds to be more easily sold. Budgets and financial management are mechanisms for accountability and control. These are also important for long-range planning, prioritizing, and operating universities. Because of the public nature of state universities, budgets and financial management may face scrutiny from the general public. Understanding the budget and the budgeting process are essential for the success of a university president. Being knowledgeable of these processes and the budget cycle of state government and the political process are crucial to securing the financial standing of a university.

CHAPTER 4

The University President's Role in the Administration's Organization

The study of administration can inform higher education. A University president can gain valuable leadership information by observing the institution's administrative apparatus. Administrative theory focuses on the total organization and attempts to develop principles that will direct managers to more efficient activities. Prominent writers in this perspective were Henri Fayol, Max Weber, and Chester Barnard. Henri Fayol (1841–1925) was a French mining engineer who spent many of his later years as an executive for a French coal and iron combine. As director of the company, Fayol authored the book, *General and Industrial Management,* in 1916. In this book, Fayol classified the study of management into several functional areas that are still commonly used in executive training and corporate development programs. Fayol identified five functional areas as the duties of the manager, planning, organizing, directing, coordinating, and controlling performance. All of these duties fall to a university president. Fayol prescribed specific principles that he had found useful during his years as a manager. He felt these principles could be used both in business organizations as well as in the government, the military, religious organizations, and financial institutions. Fayol's principles, however, were not meant to be exhaustive. Fayol's goal was to provide managers with guidelines for managerial activities. In sum, the principles emphasize efficiency, order, stability, and fairness.

These principles are still being used in modern organizations; however, these principles are not often formally used in higher education. The key to using Fayol's principles is in knowing when to apply them and how to adjust them to various situations. Fayol developed fourteen principles of management: specialization of labor that is also known as division of work, authority, discipline, unity of command, unity of direction, subordination of individual interests, remuneration, centralization, scalar chain, order, equity, personnel tenure, initiative, and esprit de corps (Harmon and Mayer, 1986, p.133). Fayol's view on management appears to be somewhat authoritarian in nature and completely management-centered. One can certainly see that some of these principles are difficult to transfer to modern higher education.

Max Weber (1864–1920) was born to a wealthy family with strong political ties in Germany. Weber was a sociologist, editor, consultant to government, and author. Weber observed the emerging forms of organization as having broad implications for managers and society. Adhering to a perspective that viewed society as becoming increasingly rational in its activities, Weber believed that organizations would become instruments of efficiency if structured around certain guidelines. In order to study this movement toward "rationality" of organizations, Weber constructed an ideal type, termed a bureaucracy that described an organization in its most rational form. Because of the emphasis on efficiency that had developed around the turn of the twentieth century, many management scholars and practitioners interpreted Weber's writings on bureaucracy as a prescription for organizing. Weber, however, was more interested in developing his bureaucratic type as a method for comparing organizational forms across societies. Although he did not believe any organization would perfectly conform to the dimensions that compose his bureaucratic model, Weber felt that some organizations would come closer than others. The closer to the bureaucratic type, the more rational society was becoming, and it was Weber's interest in the rationality of social life that directed his attention to the study of organizations.

Chester Barnard (1886–1961) used his own experiences as a manager and his extensive reading of sociological theory in constructing a theory of the organization. Barnard received a scholarship to attend Harvard University, but failed to graduate because he failed a science lab course. He still became a successful individual and rose to become the president of New Jersey Bell in 1927. Barnard's most famous work, The Functions of the Executive, viewed the organization as a "cooperative system" of individuals embodying three essential elements: willingness to cooperate, a common purpose, and communication. Barnard believed that the absence of any one of these three elements would lead to the disintegration of the organization. This system applies in today's university setting. For example, as president I meet often with the leadership team to discuss pertinent issues and to develop plans of action to implement the vision and goals of the university. We establish and reevaluate our plans based on benchmarking and best-practices. I expect the leadership team to disseminate information and to assist with the vision and goals of the university. In addition, I communicate through formal and informal channels in order to communicate effectively with the entire campus community. On the formal side, I deliver the state of the university address, I am the keynote speaker for the commencement exercises and the honors convocation twice a year, and I provide testimonies before the legislators. On the more informal side, I speak to various campus governing bodies, student groups, alumni groups, civic organizations, and religious organizations.

Barnard felt that the source of authority did not reside in the person who gave the orders. Authority resided in the subordinates who could choose either to accept or to reject directives from their superiors. Barnard also believed that employees would comply with directives when four conditions were satisfied. They could and did understand the communicated directive. They believed that the directive was consistent with the purpose of the organization. They believed that the directive was compatible with their own personal interests, and they were mentally and physically able to comply with the directive. This view of authority has become known as *acceptance theory*. I try to communicate with all employees in in a clear and personable manner. I attempt not to ever forget that these are people with feelings, emotions, and challenges; however, I am not afraid to give employees the plain truth and challenge them to a higher standard. I attempt to hold true to the university's mission and core values and make sure that any directive is consistent with the university's mission. I urge all employees to have personal ethical standards. I have a personal edict that I will not ask any employee to do something that I am not willing to do myself. Fayol's, Weber's, and Simon's concepts could certainly apply to university organizational structures.

Leadership and the University Presidency

Leadership has been defined in many different ways over the years, and there is a constant temptation to look for individuals who have the requisite skills and knowledge to become leaders. Although possessing the requisite skills may include tangible traits or characteristics, these often do not guarantee effective leadership or determine who will become an effective leader. This sentiment is also true in higher education. University presidents are searching among faculty and staff who appear to have leadership qualities and aspire to become senior-level administrators and university presidents. In looking for those who may make excellent leaders, the academic brass looks for those who may have excellent analytical abilities. They may also look for individuals with charismatic and personal style. Again, college campuses are full of these types of individuals. They may look for intelligent individuals who are able to comprehend and synthesize information quickly. Again, colleges and universities are filled with these kinds of individuals. With all of the highly intelligent individuals who teach and conduct research at universities, the exercise of searching for leaders in academia is not a science, and identifying faculty members who may have the potential to become future leaders may prove more challenging than not.

Early definitions of leadership focused on a leader who accomplished a goal by getting followers to accomplish certain goals or making followers do something by either coercion or persuasion. Early leadership theories tend to focus on personalities or certain traits of leaders. Trait leadership subscribes to a notion that there are individual attributes or characteristics or a combination of traits, behaviors, and preferences that make great leaders. Effective leaders in academia learn when to act and how to act in certain situations and with certain individuals of the university. The traits that are often focused include aspects of appearance, personality, temperament, needs, and motivation. It assumes that there are some people who are natural leaders due to certain traits not possessed by others. Leadership is not an inherited trait. It is not genetically determined like one's eye color or skin color. Typically, those who have subscribed to trait leadership have overlooked women and people of color in searching for leadership.

More modern leadership theory has shifted focus from leadership as "power over" to "power with." This shows a focus where modern leaders should focus on gaining cooperation with followers instead of dominating followers. Leaders have become conscious of the dominating undertones in the language as it relates to leaders and followers that some leaders have attempted to eliminate such words as *subordinates* and *followers* and replace them with such words as team member and *constituents*" Here, I refer to "followers" as team members. When thinking about the words *management* and *leadership*, we often intermingle the meaning of these words. Management and leadership are closely related, but they are different and the task associated with each can be different. Management often refers to the day–to-day transactions and activities that make a college or university run smoothly. Leadership often refers to a vision and uniting others toward a common goal while upholding the values of the university. Leaders can choose to utilize many different leadership styles and philosophies when carrying out their duties as a university president.

Servant Leader

The servant leader is seen as servant. This form of leadership requires us to think of the leaders as a steward in terms of relationships. The leader's relationship with others can be rated based on legacy, efficiency, effectiveness, civility, and values. Servant leadership views a leader as a servant to society and sees this position as a means to serve others. I consider myself a servant leader simply because I am in a position that requires me to serve others. I am a university president who believes in making sure that students are successful. I try to make sure that various constituencies including students, faculty, staff, parents, community members, and others have access to me when needed. One of my main goals is to inspire students to be successful and graduate; therefore, I often meet with students to discuss their challenges and their grades. I serve as a mentor for many of them. As a servant leader, I may pair them with a peer student, send them to tutoring, placing phone calls to connect individuals to the right person(s) who can assist, send them to get counseling, or simply encourage them. Although I am the chief administrator, I find it necessary to be a servant. For example, I recall meeting a student who said that he was under a lot of pressure and that his grades were not up to par. I encouraged him to stop by my office. As I expected, he did come by my office. After further inquiry with the student, I realized that he really did not have a daily study plan, and he also needed a tutor. I made a few phone calls to individuals who could help the student. I also contacted another student to serve as a peer mentor for the student. His grades ultimately improved tremendously, and he now holds a major student leadership position on campus.

Charismatic Leader

Charismatic leaders have profound influence and effects on their team members. Charismatic leaders are distinguished by their vision, their rhetorical skills, and their ability to build a particular kind of image within their followers. Charismatic leaders also have a personalized style of leadership. An example of a charismatic college president is Benjamin E. Mays, who led Morehouse College and became a mentor to Reverend Dr. Martin Luther King, Jr, while he was an undergraduate student at Morehouse. One of the most dynamic leaders with whom I had the opportunity to serve under is Dolores Spikes, former president of Southern A&M University and the University of Maryland Eastern Shore. I had the opportunity to serve in her administration at the latter institution. Although she was near the end of her career, she was very energetic and she motivated individuals. When she spoke before the university community, she always had an encouraging word that captured the attention of the audience. Because she was such a charismatic person, she was able to encourage individuals to work to their fullest potential. Under her leadership, individuals were able to balance the goals of the university while achieving their personal goals. I remember when the student enrollment had declined significantly and how Dolores Spikes was able to work with the campus and a consulting firm to create a plan that generated the largest freshman classes for three consecutive years. Dolores Spikes was the kind of leader who was very persuasive. In essence, she was a great orator who did most of her speaking impromptu and spoke directly to the issues at hand while making individuals believe that they were included and had the capacity to make a difference.

Transformational Leader

Transformational leadership focuses on the ongoing relationship between leaders and team members. Transformational leadership occurs when leaders motivate others to do more than they originally intended and often more than they thought possible. The transformational model highlights a leader's ability to lead team members to become better people and thus better employees. These leaders motivate colleagues and team members to view their work from a new perspective and embrace the mission and vision of the university. According to Bass and Avolio (1990), these leaders influence and motivate people through the four I's; idealized influence, inspirational motivation, intellectual stimulation, and individualized consideration. This type of leadership often occurs when there are changes in the culture and organization of a university.

I have often been intrigued by one of my mentors, Freeman Hrabowski, president of the University of Maryland Baltimore County (UMBC). I had the opportunity to serve as an American Council on Education (ACE) Fellow under his leadership. He reaches out to individuals and encourages them to achieve greatness. He reminds all of those who he mentors of the importance of giving back to the community and those less fortunate. In essence, he has been able to get faculty, staff, students, leaders, and many other individuals to make a difference in higher education and in society. Under Freeman's leadership, UMBC became an honors university in Maryland. This university is now renowned for STEM programs and research in science, technology, mathematics, and engineering. Through his charisma and hard work, he obtained a generous donation from the Myerhoff family and started the Myerhoff Scholars program that initially started with African American males and later included African American females, and now includes students from all races. He increased a diverse population of academically inclined students who graduate and attend some of the most prestigious colleges and universities in the nation. These students pursue such degrees such as Ph.D.s, MDs, JDs, and many others.

Academic Leaders

Those who become effective leaders in academia must have a vision to set the university's goals. These individuals also hold the interpersonal skills to achieve consensus and the verbal capacity to communicate with enthusiasm to large diverse groups (i.e., faculty, staff, students, alumni, business community, and the community at large). These individuals also have the capacity to coordinate the disparate efforts of the university. Most of all, these individuals desire to lead. They are not afraid of taking the helm of leadership and making tough decisions and taking a risk when necessary. Academic leadership has a purpose. It is to guide colleges and universities that will facilitate change in society and thus the betterment of society. Academic leaders who hold these positions must look for those who desire to lead and assist them in developing as leaders. Academia should continue to produce leaders who inspire, set goals, and stand for something. University employees (team members) have great expectations of their president. They expect the university president to be honest, responsible, and fair. They expect the president to be forward-thinking, but most of all they expect them to be authentic. Authentic leadership is born out of one's heart. The university presidency is more than strategic planning (though this is vital to success of any university). The university presidency involves values first and results second. Results are important because if one does not get results, the individual will not have a long tenure as a university president. An authentic university president does not merely give the command to "work." Authentic leaders are willing to roll up their sleeves and work along with others. University leadership is about relationships and earning the trust of those who are employed at the college or university. As a university president, an individual must earn the respect of employees so that they buy in to the vision of long-term success for the university. After my first year as president, members of the Board of Trustees stated that I was underpaid and thereby suggested that I be given an increase in salary. They wanted to make my salary competitive with that of peer institutions. I therefore stated that my increase could not exceed that of other individuals on campus. I wanted individuals to know that I was willing to sacrifice salary until times got better. I informed the Board members that all other university employees were getting a 2.5% increase, and therefore I would only accept the same salary increase as the provost, deans, chairs, faculty, and all other university employees.

Provost

One of the key academic leaders is the provost. The original meaning for the term *provost* was the "keeper of prisons." The Provost Marshal of the Norman invaders in 1066 was infamous for torture and merciless cruelty. Suspected deserters and drunks during the American Revolution were very poorly treated in their respective "provost prisons." There has not been exact documentation when the term "provost" was first used in education. During the late eighteenth century and early nineteenth century, two universities began to use the term. In the 1930s, the University of Pennsylvania's trustee board created the position by separating the duties from the duties of the university's president. The provost became the chief academic officer, but the office fell below the presidency on the hierarchal chart. At Columbia University, the Board of Trustees established the office of provost in 1811. In universities, the provost is the second-ranking officer in the administrative hierarchy. According to the Higher Ed Jobs website, the average salary for a provost in the United States is $132,575.

The provost serves at the pleasure of the university president and can be removed by the university president. The provost may also serve as acting chief executive officer during a vacancy of the university president. The provost typically has ten years or more of experience in academia and has achieved the rank of at least an associate professor. The provost's duties are to oversee and advance the interests of undergraduate, graduate, and professional programs at the university. The provost advocates for academic priorities and makes sure to recruit and retain a diverse faculty. The provost is the marshal of resources in support of excellent teaching, research and creative activity, and service. The provost develops academic policies and programs for a college or university and directs and coordinates activities of deans and chairpersons of individual colleges. The provost provides oversight for personnel matters and determines scheduling of courses and recommends implementation of additional courses. Tenure and promotion decisions come from departments and ultimately come to the Office of the Provost for final approval. As provost of Western Illinois University, I served under President Al Goldfarb. We had one of the best working relationships that any president and provost could have. We were always able to discuss the business of the university in a very open and amicable way. In his absence, I was able to represent him at many functions and to carry out his plans. In addition, he served not just as a colleague and supervisor, but as a mentor and friend. This kind of relationship developed over a period of time and it was based on trust and honesty. We were able to discuss the challenges that we both faced in leadership positions.

Academic Deans

Another key administrative leader at a university is the academic dean. The meaning of "dean" comes from "a leader of ten," which was taken from medieval monasteries. The monks were organized into groups of ten for administrative purposes with a "decanus," a senior monk leading the unit. The term was later used to denote the head of a community of priests, as the chapter of a cathedral, or a section of a diocese the "deanery." Deans, especially if they rise from the ranks at the school where they were a faculty member, must transition from operating as an individual and leading a department to looking at the bigger picture. In addition, deans are called upon to gain consensus and cooperation from departments on decisions affecting their colleges. In becoming an academic dean, there must be a transition from focusing solely on one's department or discipline to focusing on one's college and overall university's vision and goals. Academic deans must balance the needs of the college with the needs of the institution. They serve as spokespersons and advocates for the institutional perspective while communicating their particular college's needs to the provost and president. The academic dean must become familiar with all of the various disciplines that fall within the college. For example, in a College of Liberal Arts, an academic unit might consist of such departments as history, philosophy, fine art, English, theatre, music, and foreign languages. All of these disciplines are vastly different, and the research, teaching, and tenure expectations are different in each discipline. Academic deans must familiarize themselves with all of the disciplines that fall within the college. One needs not be an expert, but be familiar with each discipline because it will provide one with credibility.

Department Chairs

It has been quoted in academic circles that the "department chair" position is the most difficult position on the academic ladder because it is the classic middle management position. Departments within the university have a department chair who is a faculty member usually appointed or selected by an academic dean. Department chairs often have to find a positive balance between the upper administration, faculty, and students. Department chairs must continue to pursue their research agenda's while balancing administrative duties, teaching duties, and service duties. When combined with balancing a personal life these can prove to be difficult. Even with these potential difficulties, department chairs are pivotal to the advancement of the university's teaching, research, and service. In addition, department chairs are essential to a university's efforts to enhance the diversity and the intellectual climate of the campus. The department chair is often an underappreciated individual who is a part of the university's leadership.

A chair, like other administrators, often attempts to become all things to all people; however, this can cause administrators to become exhausted and soon burn out. Department chairs must balance the needs of the discipline with the needs of the institution, and they serve as spokespersons and advocates for the institutional perspective and the communicator for their particular college's needs. Department chairs who cannot shift to supporting the institution's perspective when necessary will find it very difficult to fulfill their institutional leadership role.

In a complex bureaucratic structure such as the university, it can sometimes be unclear of the authority that a department chair holds. Chairs oversee the day-to-day operations of departments and within this can talk with faculty about teaching, research, and advisement. Department chairs field student complaints against faculty members and are the first in the administrative hierarchy. If complaints are not handled correctly on this level, they may become a problem for the upper administration. From time to time, it may be necessary for the university president to hold discussions with department chairs to gain a different perspective of the university. In some cases, the university president becomes insular to particular segments of the university and meetings with the provost and deans provide only one perspective. Most university presidents rely primarily on the provost and academic vice president and the academic deans for information; however, periodic meetings with department chairs can be quite informative. Department chairs meet regularly with the faculty and students and, therefore, can inform the president of vital campus issues. To be successful as a department chair, chairs must be familiar with the resources that are available.

Staff

Administrative assistants and other staff on university campuses are often undervalued; however, these individuals are vital to the overall operation and success of the university. Any wise university president understands the importance of all individuals who are a part of the campus workforce. A university president must develop stable and cordial relationships with everyone. When the president develops and maintains these types of relationships with everyone, it creates an atmosphere of trust, respect, and mutual understanding. Individuals need to believe that they can talk openly with the president and other administrators about vital issues regarding the university. The abuse of power should not be a perception of the office of the president. At Western Illinois University, I am simply known as Jack. This is less formal than many universities. Faculty, staff, and administrators refer to me by first name. One of my friends came to visit me and he could not believe that people were calling me "Jack." He thought it was a sign of disrespect, but it is the culture of Western that administrators are usually called by their first names.

External Forces in Higher Education

There are many challenges facing higher education. The high costs and the amount of debt incurred by parents and students are staggering. I speak both as a university president and as the father of two sons in college. By 2020, four years at a top-tier school will cost $328,000; by 2028 the estimated cost is $589,000; and by 2035 a college education will cost an astonishing $788,000. Parents and students are already taking on considerable debt to finance education. In 2011, student debt surpassed credit card debt for the first time. These growing costs and debt associated with higher education are unsustainable.

In many cases, universities are not preparing college students for life after graduation and the workforce. In many American colleges and universities, there are currently too many overly specialized niche courses that have no practical application to employment. There should be access to liberal arts education so that students can gain an appreciation, but all university courses should have a practical component to them. There should be more collaborative efforts among departments. For example, Western Illinois University offers a course that is cross-listed with three departments: African American Studies, Women's Studies, and Sociology. The course is titled, "Race, Class, and Gender." The course is offered during the summer session and is team taught by professors from all three disciplines. Within universities, colleges, departments, and divisions, programs are too often operated independently. All entities within a university must begin to search for ways to meet common institutional goals.

CHAPTER 5

Faculty Life and the University Presidency

In many instances, the working relationship between the faculty and the upper-level administration has been characterized as one that is filled with tension. This kind of working relationship is not optimal, nor is it helpful or healthy for the advancement of the University's mission. The president and the faculty must work together to promote a healthy working relationship across campus and in the university community. It is important for the university president to create various opportunities for dialogue where he or she can communicate a vision, values, and goals to the faculty and all constituents.

Labor Unions and the University

The recent battles of labor unions in Wisconsin and Ohio and the public sector employees have brought new attention to unions at public universities, but the growth of unions for white collar employees saw substantial growth during the 1970s and 1980s (Aronwitz, 1998). During this time, unionized faculties on college campuses became more prominent. In 1995, approximately 40% of all full-time faculty in the United States were represented by labor unions (Julius & Gumport, 2002). Unions have also expanded to include adjunct and part-time faculty (Bodah, 2000). This trend has even trickled down to the graduate student populations. In the late 1990s and early 2000s, graduate students and graduate research assistants at twenty-three American universities voted to unionize, and graduate student employees at approximately nineteen other institutions attempted to unionize (Rhoads & Rhoades, 2005). In 2011, the University of Illinois at Chicago organized and voted to organize a faculty union, which was the first formed at a major research university in Illinois since the 1970s.

Western Illinois University unionized as one of the five Board of Governor Universities (BGU) schools (WIU, Eastern Illinois University, Chicago State, Governor's State, and Northeastern Illinois University) in the early 1970's. The union (AFT/IFT/ University Professionals of Illinois or UPI) took hold largely because of a very unpopular merit system put in place at the time. In 1996, the BGU disbanded and Western formed its own board of trustees and negotiated its first contract with Western chapter of UPI. Both sides committed to "principled" negotiations (popularized in the book *Getting to Yes*) and successfully negotiated an Agreement accepted enthusiastically by both sides. Subsequent contracts or agreements have been negotiated with the same level of cooperation and the relationship between the administration and union leaders has a history of being very positive at Western.

I come from a working class family, and I support labor unions. I recognize that unions can help improve the working conditions for laborers and provide them with more job satisfaction. I understand the relationship between the administration and the union may be adversarial by the way it is constructed and has traditionally operated. I understand that as president of the university, I am seen as part of the establishment, which at times seems odd to me especially when my personal view of myself is that as a man of the people. This does not prevent me from making the best decisions for the university as a whole. At times, it is challenging to work with the union leadership as I have to think of the entire institution and all its stakeholders while the union leadership has a much narrower range of interests. I have worked to be transparent in all that I do regarding the decisions that have to be made. I consider ideas and listen to suggestions from union leaders and members with regard to the challenges we face. I meet regularly with the union, host town hall meetings on the budget and other topics, and do all that I can to arrive at consensus with the union leaders for solutions to problems. In Illinois, we have had major reductions to our funding from the state in recent years, and we have managed to negotiate the extension or spreading out of pay raises on two occasions resulting in significant savings in resources for the essential needs of the university. In return for the union leaders' willingness to support these agreements, the university leadership has committed to no lay-offs or furloughs, new opportunities for faculty to participate in grants and research projects, and to avoid significant cuts in programs, if possible. The good will that had been established since the first contract in 1996 helped to ensure the cooperation that was needed for the financial stability of our institution. Openness, transparency, willingness to listen and compromise, and enlightened union leadership all contributed to getting us through a fiscal crises.

At Western Illinois University, the provost meets, confers, and negotiates in good faith with the union, which represents faculty, staff, technical, and clerical employees. The labor agreement between the union and the university defines wages, hours, and terms of condition of employment. On university campuses, some departments are more prestigious than others, and some faculty are more prestigious than others. Business professors typically are paid more than liberal arts professors because it is perceived that business professors can pursue higher paying jobs in the private sector. Professors who bring large amounts of money into the university through grants and contracts are perceived to be more esteemed than adjunct professors, assistant professors, and even other senior professors. Another reality of the professorship in higher education is that the job is less demanding than a K–12 teaching position. Last, failure to get tenure is a constant reality on the minds of young and untenured faculty. Research expectations at some universities have grown so demanding and the pressure to "publish or perish" has become so prevalent that many young faculty members may find greater satisfaction at a different kind of university. I would estimate that about one fourth to one half of all tenure-track faculty do not obtain tenure and are dismissed from their positions.

Faculty Development

In the university setting, faculty development has been used to describe sabbaticals, research grants, and funding to attend professional meetings. Some universities have expanded the definition to include a wider range of activities, such as fellowships, curriculum design, teaching skills (face to face and on-line), presentation skills, technology skills, and interpersonal skills. Faculty development should assist and support faculty in their professional development. Faculty development can range from how to use the latest technology in classes to how to teach a particular subject effectively.

All faculty members, those who are new, seasoned, tenured, and untenured should have a faculty development plan. This plan should have a multiyear list of professional goals and activities that will assist in faculty development. Faculty members should periodically check and evaluate their own progress toward obtaining their goals. This is not a contract or a part of your formal contract with the university or your annual evaluations conducted by your department chair, but it will allow you to stay focused on what activities and action that will take place over a three to seven year period of faculty member's academic career. The faculty development should be discussed with your chair or dean to ensure that the bar has not been set too high or too low. A well-thought-out faculty development plan can be a blueprint for success.

Universities should organize formal faculty development programs. Most universities have a unit that is responsible for effective teaching or a unit to assist in faculty growth and development. These units may be most effective at the departmental level where the faculty member is in close proximity with senior faculty of their department. A senior faculty member can be instrumental in assisting the young faculty member in refining their research agenda, sharpening their teaching skills, and navigating through the maze of university, college, and departmental politics. A formal faculty development program can assist senior professors with the change in student populations and the nature and culture of the new college student in America. As campuses become more diverse, formal faculty development can be the mechanism to assist students in reaching their full intellectual capacity regardless of their race, gender, sexual preference, or nontraditional status. I have found mentoring young faculty to be a sound form of faculty development. I confer with my ACE fellow mentors, Freeman Hrabowski and Dolores Spikes, regularly. In addition, I consult with the previous president, Al Goldfarb, on issues that may involve institutional history.

Faculty Governance and the University President

The nature of faculty work has traditionally included responsibility for some aspects of governance of the university. This governance is usually through the faculty senate and through university-wide, college-wide, and departmental committees. Although committee service work is an expectation of all faculty members, new faculty should limit the number of committees they serve on during the early part of their careers. First year and reasonably new faculty should be spared of committee work because some committee decisions are political in nature, and new faculty should get acclimated to the politics of a university before taking part in such decision making. Similar to committee work within the Congress, some committees at universities are perceived as powerful, whereas others are not. Some of the most powerful committees at a university are typically the curriculum committee, personnel committee, and budgetary committee, but this may vary depending on the university. Committee work does provide opportunities for new faculty to meet faculty and administrators outside of their departments and establish a broader presence to those within the university. It is important for both new and seasoned faculty members to remember that committee work does count as service, and service is a component of tenure and promotions and other merit-based raises. At most universities, similar to Western Illinois University, the faculty senate is recognized as the official voice of faculty members. I meet regularly with our faculty senate and consult with the leadership on my goals and objectives each year. I also have established a President's Roundtable, consisting of faculty of various ranks, who provide important feedback to me on my initiatives throughout the year. The President's Roundtable also discusses concerns that arise regarding maintaining all aspects of the academic enterprise.

Faculty Tenure and Promotion

Faculty members should understand the terms of their employment. Even in right-to-work states, tenure and promotion processes at universities have remained a mainstay in the conditions of employment and academic life for professors. There has been much scholarly work on faculty rights, and these rights vary from university to university. There are some universal principles and practices that are accepted by most American universities. Newly hired faculty should have a clear statement of the terms of appointment. The faculty contract should state the period of time, the expected teaching and research assignment, overtime load (if necessary), advisement and other advisory responsibilities, and the right to engage in outside employment. Faculty members also have the right to expect teaching assignments within their areas of professional competencies or reasonable notice of a new course assignment, and faculty members should receive a written statement indicating any credit granted toward tenure (usually between two and three years). Tenure and promotion in rank is a holistic determination based on the totality of the faculty member's accomplishments. At most universities, the primary criteria for tenure and promotion is production of peer-reviewed scholarship and/or creative works and a demonstrable record of service. Each department at the university sets the promotion and tenure criteria to reflect the expectations of the disciplines represented in the department.

Faculty should also expect to be evaluated periodically by their chair and/or departmental faculty committee. These reviews are essential in making faculty aware of their progress toward tenure and/or promotion. If there are deficiencies, this allows them to refine their faculty development plan and overcome any weaknesses that may prohibit them from obtaining tenure and promotion. Members of the faculty also deserve a fair and impartial decision in tenure and promotion. If tenure is denied, they deserve to be shown the reasons based on clearly stated departmental criteria. A faculty member should have received the proper advanced notice when the decision is made not to grant tenure; however, the faculty member also has the right to appeal to the higher authority in administrative hierarchy if they believe that they have received unfair treatment. If a tenure and promotion decision reaches the university president's level, then the decision should be examined, although the decision would most likely stand unless there have been some egregious and nefarious action taken at a lower level.

Academic Freedom and the University President

Academic freedom is the right of a faculty member to discuss or investigate any controversial social, economic, or political issues without interference or penalty from the university administration and public officials. Academic freedom allows freedom of inquiry and is rooted in the First Amendment rights of the United States Constitution at public universities. Academic freedom allows one to express public statements and ideas or distribute controversial information without fear that recourse or punitive action will be taken against the faculty making the statement. Academic freedom is not permission or the right of a faculty member to have the expectation of individual autonomy to say and do whatever one likes.

Academicians have not always enjoyed this freedom. In October 1903, John Spencer Bassett, a professor at Duke University (the Trinity College), offered praise to Booker T. Washington, who was an African American leader, in a public setting (Porter, 1972). He also addressed these issues in his scholarly publications. In his analysis, Bassett advocated that there should be vocational education for the masses (Porter, 1972). This was consistent with Washington's philosophy. Bassett also advocated that there should be cultural education for the few, which was the view of DuBois (Porter, 1972). Bassett also believed that if southern whites saw former slaves as human beings, they would have provided them with better educational opportunities. Bassett's accolades for the philosophies of two black leaders drew regional and national attention (Porter, 1972). The fallout and ensuing controversy became known as the "Bassett Affair" (Porter, 1972). Bassett's views and his article garnered criticism from white conservative Southern leaders (Porter, 1972). They began a campaign and called for Bassett's dismissal. By December 1903, the entire faculties of the college threatened to resign if Bassett was not let go (Porter, 1972). The board of trustees did not succumb to the pressure and Bassett did not resign (Porter, 1972). This is an early case of academic freedom that shows that faculty can speak without fear reprisals for comments by university presidents. University classrooms are not "bully pulpits" where professors "force-feed" students personal opinions unrelated to the subject matter of the course. Understanding of the concept of academic freedom is an obligation of the faculty member and should be clearly articulated and distinguished from matters of university policy, so all will be aware of what academic freedom is and is not. Whereas faculty members can disagree with a policy, this does not mean that they can simply ignore the policy. Academic freedom does not protect faculty members from non-university penalties if they break the law, nor does it protect an incompetent teacher or those who repeatedly do not teach the subject matter or repeatedly cancel class. In violating all of the preceding, the faculty member could be subject to separation from the institution.

Faculty members have the right to criticize academic programs, administrative policies, and procedures within the university. When this occurs, I want viable recommendations if faculty should disagree with policies and procedures. When and if faculty members speak out of their personal, political, or religious beliefs, one must be mindful of the tenor of civility and decency of the discussion which are cornerstone pieces of academia. Faculty members have the right to engage in any pursuits as long as those pursuits do not interfere with their faculty duties or terms of employment. Depending on the comments and with the wide reach of social and traditional media, this can be a source of embarrassment for the university.

Presidential Advice for Future Faculty

I have mentored many graduate students who have asked me various questions regarding academic life on college and university campuses. Many of their long-term goals include becoming a senior-level administrator and possibly a university president. I typically advise them to pursue the traditional route to the presidency. The traditional route, in my opinion, involves coming up through the ranks of the faculty. This process begins when newly designated doctoral graduates accept their first tenure-track faculty positions. Although the president is not directly involved with the recruitment process for hiring faculty, it is imperative that the president is aware of the process. When it has been decided that a faculty hire will take place, there typically should be approval to hire by the provost, academic dean, and chair. The chair must decide what specialization in the department needs to be filled. If it is a simple replacement of an existing faculty member, then simply replacing the vacated position is the most viable option. If it is a newly created position, then the chair must determine what specialty is needed in the department. Again, this may come from accreditation requirements, discipline experts, or student demands. For example, if the Department of Literature has an opening, the chair must determine to hire a faculty member in a specific area of the discipline or hire a generalist who can serve in multiple and varied courses.

The chair must also determine if the knowledge, skills, and abilities will be listed in the advertisement. Most academic vacancies are advertised in the *Chronicle of Higher Education, HigherEd Jobs, Diverse Magazine, Outlook,* and others. Many disciplines hold preliminary interviews at annual association meetings. The university president has very little to do with faculty advertisement, the university's human resource department, academic dean, and provost handle the details of advertising and hiring faculty.

Prospective faculty members should be aware of the faculty interview process. This process is fundamentally different from interviewing for a job outside of the academy. This interview process or some variation is used in most academic positions. The interview for a university presidency functions somewhat differently and that process will be discussed in a later chapter. Most universities use a search committee. This group usually consists of faculty members from the department with the vacancy and may be a student representative who is majoring in the discipline.

When on-campus interviews are set, those who are not serving on the search committee are asked to review the credentials of the applicants. The on-campus interview is usually a one–to–three–day process consisting of group meetings with various individuals from the department and other individuals on the campus. Candidates receive a proposed agenda prior to their arrival. During the on–campus interview, one–on–one meetings are usually scheduled with individual faculty. Small group interviews are scheduled with faculty. Group meetings are scheduled with students, and a research presentation and teaching demonstration are typically required. There is also usually a public forum or social gathering where applicants can meet with students and members of the community and a campus tour. Candidates are generally asked about research interests, professional goals, teaching strategies, and the reason(s) they applied for the position. Other questions may include, "How can your strengths and expertise become an asset to our department?" "How would you handle an incident of academic misconduct?" and "List weaknesses that you wish to improve on?"

It is important that a job candidate spend time practicing the research presentation for speaking delivery, tone, and pace. Check all handouts and power points for typographical errors. Be enthusiastic during the presentation and show the faculty that you have mastered the topic covered in the presentation. After the presentation, there is usually a question and answer period. Never be afraid to say, I do not know. Poorly done research presentations and teaching demonstrations will weigh very heavily in faculty opinions of you and could affect your ranking against other candidates. Prepare your presentation as if you were presenting at a professional meeting. In addition, during the on-campus interview, take extra copies of up–to-date curriculum vitae and any of your recent publications.

Before going to an on-campus interview, go on the department website and spend time learning about the faculty members in the department. Learn their teaching interests, research interests, and any other information that the website may provide about the department. This will allow you to develop and ask well-designed and in-depth inquiries during the interview. Being aware of the research interests of faculty in the department may help candidates to ask substantive questions during the interview. After the on-campus interviews with all applicants are conducted, the faculty members of the department share their opinions about the candidates in a group meeting. After this discussion, in many cases a faculty vote is conducted to determine the top candidate for the vacancy; however, in some instances, the chair of the search committee may ask the committee members to provide a list of strengths and weaknesses.

Sometimes, there can be spirited discussions over who the best candidate is and where the other applicants rank. If this is the case, it is imperative for the chair of the selection committee to distill all of the information and build a consensus. In most cases, the search committee recommends and ranks the top three candidates to the academic dean for final selections. The academic dean extends the offer letter to the candidate, who usually has a period of time to accept or decline the offer. If a suitable candidate is not found, the search committee may go back to the pool or close the search and wait until the next academic year and begin a new search. These offers are usually not written in stone and an administration may entertain reasonable counteroffers from individuals with many years of experience. If hard dollars cannot be offered, start-up packages including graduate student assistance, particular software, release time, special travel budgets, or some other resource may be requested. At some universities, academic rank can also negotiated as part of the process. In faculty searches, a university president virtually has little or no contact at all with job candidates. At some small colleges, an applicant may meet the university president, but this is highly unlikely.

CHAPTER 6

Student Affairs and the University Presidency

Students are the lifeblood of any university. Without students, universities would cease to exist. Universities vary in size and scope. In 2010, Arizona State University enrolled 56,562 undergraduate students and the University of Central Florida enrolled 47,580 undergraduate students, whereas Edgewood College enrolled 1,941 undergraduates, Stillman College had an enrollment of 1,116 students, the Ohio State University enrolled more than 50,145, and Yale University enrolled 5,310 undergraduates (NCES, 2011). These statistics provide a bird's-eye view of the enrollment trends at some of the nation's largest and smallest institutions. Regardless of the size of an institution, many American colleges and universities will experience some student behavioral issues that must be addressed by institutional personnel.

Undergraduate Students and Student Behavior

Undergraduate education is the entry education level taken to earn a baccalaureate degree. Traditional undergraduate students usually fall within the eighteen-to-twenty-four-year-old age demographic, and pursuit of an undergraduate degree for full-time students traditionally takes four years to complete. It appears, however, that this time has been expanded and in many cases has become a five–to-six year process for some undergraduate students. At one time, universities acted in *loco parentis* for their students (Thelin, 2011), meaning in the place of the parents, but this is no longer true. For the most part, students experience their freedoms during their college years.

By far the most common usage of in *loco parentis* relates to faculty and students. For hundreds of years, the English common-law concept shaped the rights and responsibilities of public school teachers: until the late nineteenth century, their legal authority over students was as broad as that of parents. Changes in American education and a broader court interpretation of the rights of students forced changes by the 1960s. In addition, cultural changes brought a resurgence of the doctrine in the twenty-first century. The individual from my leadership team who has the most contact with undergraduate students is the vice president for student services. The nature of student affairs' work allows the vice president of student services to administrate and adjudicate with student disciplinary problems and student misconduct. Although these responsibilities are among the chief responsibilities of the vice president of student affairs, these duties are not the sole authority of this position. In all cases, due process must be adhered.

With undergraduate students, misconduct usually includes destroying or defacing school property, academic dishonesty, and showing a lack of adherence to academic policy. The most notable misconduct that I have witnessed over the last few years is the number of underage drinking cases at college campuses in the United States. The consumption of alcoholic beverages on college campuses has become an indelible part of undergraduate social life. There have been traditions, songs, and games built around drinking on college campuses, and overtime drinking has become a socialized aspect of life there. In the United States, the legal drinking age is twenty-one, and undergraduate students under the age of twenty-one must adhere to that rule or face the consequences, which may be dire. The kinds of conduct that cause most students to be expelled comes from outside of the classroom and academic sphere as they are usually cases of sexual misconduct, underage drinking, drug use, or other disorderly behavior.

Most universities have a student court or a committee whereby a student accused of misconduct can receive due process and have their case adjudicated. These committees should be composed of both faculty and students, and this group usually has the power to hand down sanctions and suspensions. These kinds of community tribunals can also be used in the residence hall communities. It is best for universities to give students a role in disciplinary matters. Institutional policies guiding student conduct must be reasonable or students will reject these policies. A famous case from the 1960s involved six students who were expelled from Alabama State University (then college), by the Alabama State Board of Education and the president of the university, H. C. Trenholm, (Shekleton, 2009). The students were expelled for participating in lunch counter desegregation sit-ins at local cafeterias. It is true as with most Southern state governors of that era, used a heavy hand in dealing with black college presidents. Trenholm was urged by the governor to "get the ring leaders" and "...expel the students who participated in mass demonstration for civil rights." It is clear that President Trenholm participated in expelling the students out of fear of retaliation from the governor (Shekleton, 2009). The students filed suit in federal court. The court held that the students were expelled without due process and did not have the opportunity to defend themselves against the charges. Adherence to due process and student privacy are two policies that govern student behavior and conduct at all universities.

Universities must adhere to the Family Educational and Privacy Act of 1974 (FERPA) also known as the Buckley Act. This law gave students access to their education records and an opportunity to seek to have the records amended. This law also gives students some control over the disclosure of information from their university records. With several exceptions, universities must have a student's permission prior to the disclosure of educational records. The law only applies to educational agencies and institutions that receive funding under a program administered by the U.S. Department of Education. FERPA should be abandoned when there is a clear and present danger to the students.

Student Orientation

In many instances, today's student orientation is a two- or three-day process consisting of activities that introduce new students to the university. During the new student orientation process, students are given tools that will help them to acclimate to a university or college campus. One of the primary functions of orientation is to make students realize that college is much different than high school. This is where students get the first opportunity to witness the new standard of intellectualism that is expected at a university. Another purpose of orientation is to introduce new students and their families to the services and resources offered by the university.

Common elements of an orientation include making arrangements for housing, learning the campus and the city or town, learning about campus groups, learning about Greek organizations, registering for classes, and participating in social events. During orientation sessions, students can take their placement exams, declare their major, and register for fall courses. There are strengths in numbers and orientation is an opportunity for the new student to meet new people and to make new friends to have on their journey through their college years. Students who attend orientation programs together may form an unofficial cohort that may be helpful when one is trying to cope with the challenges of the first-year collegiate experience. A recent trend shows that colleges are making orientation a one-stop shop where students can complete orientation in one day; however, a typical orientation program includes a minimum of one night's stay. Orientation services work closely with the office of admission. At some universities they fall under the same division. The role of the university president during orientation is to provide students with a welcome to the university and meet and greet any families that may have accompanied their child to orientation. During these interactions with new students and their families, it is best to convey the seriousness of higher education and relay your expectation as the university president. This allows the university president to set the tone for a successful academic year.

For example, one year at the new student convocation I gave a speech where I articulated the expectations of the university and what it means to be a successful college student. I specifically spoke about being a professional student and making the transition from high school to college life. During my address, I emphasized that individuals should not wear saggy pants, du-rags outside of their rooms, nor should they wear pajamas and flip-flops to class, nor engage in other socially unacceptable presentations of self. Later, I saw a young man wearing saggy pants, and he was walking with his parents. I immediately approached him and asked him if he heard my address where I mentioned the saggy pants. He was apologetic and indicated that he would dress appropriately from that point forward. Orientation is an excellent opportunity to set the tone for the academic year, and this can often begin with the university president.

Student Evaluations

Student evaluations of university faculty began during the 1960s in the academy. Since that time, colleges and universities have seen this trend spread to most American universities. The key question in dealing with student evaluations is, "Are they a valid and reliable measure of effective teaching?" It has long been argued that these evaluations play too great a role in whether a professor receives tenure and promotion in the academy. Poor student evaluations can cause adjunct professors to be removed from the classroom immediately. Any tenure review that is based solely on student evaluations is an inappropriate use of the evaluation tool. Student evaluations should be only a part of the total evaluation for tenure and promotions. Student evaluations should be used in conjunction with peer evaluations. There is also a likely correlation between good students' ratings and professors who are easy graders or friendly. Likewise, if students perceived course work is difficult or they are not interested in the course work, it is more probable that the professor may receive a poor evaluation. In any event, a professor should never lower the academic standard for course expectations to receive better student evaluations.

RateMyProfessor.com is a new form of student evaluations. It is not sanctioned by universities. The site was originally launched as TeacherRatings.com and converted to RateMyProfessor.com in 2001. In 2005, Patrick Nagle and William DeSantis bought RateMyProfessors.com, and they later sold the site to Viacom (which owns television networks that air programming that targets an eighteen-to-twenty-four- year-old demographic) in 2007. RateMyProfessors. com has become the largest online destination for professor ratings. According to RateMyProfessors.com, their database holds over 14 million student comments and ratings, 7,500 universities, and 1.7 million professors from colleges and universities across the United States, Canada, and the United Kingdom. The "Highest Rated" professors and "Hottest" professors are also listed. Students have increasingly used this site in making decisions of which professors to take and which to avoid. For most tenured professors, the site is a nonfactor, and they really do not believe the ratings can have a negative or positive impact on whether they are tenured and promoted. For junior faculty who are not tenured, the site has become a method for gathering information that cannot be found in the formal university student evaluations (i.e. an opinion on how attractive one may look).

Student Publications

The student newspaper is a formidable symbol of the First Amendment and a voice in a university. The first student newspaper arguably began at Dartmouth College in 1799, and has grown since that time; however, Boudoin, Cornell, Harvard, Miami, Ohio Wesleyan, Simpson, and Yale also claim to have published the first student newspaper publication in the country (College Media Matters, 2013). From its inception, the student newspaper was simply an extension of the university's public relations entity. Today, student newspapers have advisors, student journalists, student editors, and a line item in most university budgets. The student newspaper should cover all events on campus, distinguished speakers and lecturers, and cultural and social events. The student newspaper and other publications provide experience for student writers who have not had the opportunity to gain work experience. Most student editors and writers are passionate, and they want the student newspaper to be the true student voice. In doing so, editors and writers can become overzealous in coverage of certain aspects of campus life. It is the duty of the student newspaper to report accurately and objectively particular concerns of the students and the institution. The newspaper can editorialize on pertinent subjects and should strive toward excellence in doing so. The student newspaper can damage or improve the image of the university. If there is an onslaught of negative stories about the university and/or community, it could affect the university's efforts in the community and state and local governments.

The student newspaper should have a faculty advisor and an advisory board made up of students and faculty. The faculty advisor should be someone experienced in working with student journalists and be familiar with the code of ethics that guide student newspaper advisors. There should be policies, guidelines, or constitutions in place to govern student publications. Many student journalists may balk at such policies believing that it is a form of censorship; however, the university president is responsible for all aspects of the university, and the top priority is to lead the university and to protect the university's academic reputation and brand. It must be stressed to student journalists that they must adhere to their own moral codes but operate in a responsible manner, realizing that every story is not a "Watergate Scandal." Censorship should not be the goal of a university president or the university; however, the institution is responsible for helping students to develop a code of ethics and responsibility that will guide their decision making. Universities historically attempt to avoid the appearance of censorship; however, institutions must make sure that they are covered in the cases of libel, slander, and obscenity. In these cases, it may be necessary to censor the newspaper to protect the university. There should be a balance of coverage in student newspapers. There are usually four main parts of a student newspaper: news, features, sports, and editorials. Controversies usually stem from articles written in the news section or editorial section.

In recent years, there have been some well-publicized quarrels over the role and operations of student newspapers. In 2007, the administration at Grambling State University decided to shut down production of *The Gramblinite*, the student newspaper (Cardinal Points Online, 2007). The administration stated that it wanted to provide "quality assurance" of the newspaper. The provost sent a memorandum to the newspaper staff informing them that the newspaper was "suspended" until the university officials could better control the paper's quality.

Grambling's administration believed they could suspend the newspaper's production based on the ruling in *Hosty v. Carter* decision in 2005. In that decision, the Seventh U.S. Circuit Court of Appeals ruled that limited freedom of expression rights applicable to high school newspapers could be extended to college campuses. Grambling's move to suspend the paper was a strong and bold move; however, it may have violated a court ruling in Sixth Circuit Court of Appeals case from *Kincaid v. Gibson* in 2001 (Lisby, 2002). In this case, the court ruled that Kentucky State University administrators could not confiscate copies of the student yearbook due to "poor quality" and an "inappropriate" theme (Lisby, 2002). This move may have caused Grambling more problems than it solved because of the perception that the school was censoring the student newspaper.

In 2010, the student government president at the University of Kansas proposed that the university cut funding for the student newspaper because of a perceived inappropriate relationship between the student senate and the student newspaper (College Media Matters, 2010). The student newspaper was accused of an inability to report objectively on the student senate meetings. The president proposed that $1.70 be cut from the $4.00 student media fee. This cut is representative of the amount that pays for the newspaper staff's salaries and subsidizes a free copy of the daily paper for all members of the student body. In the end, the student senate voted down the proposal and it was defeated (College Media Matters, 2010). This example illustrates the importance of student newspapers as a vehicle for the students' voices.

Printing newspapers can be costly for institutions and can involve complex situations that must be given careful consideration. Universities usually do not have their own facilities to print the university newspapers. Many student newspapers are funded in total or in part by the university and supplemented by revenue from advertising sales. Funding is usually taken up by printing costs. In most cases, it is cheaper to contract out printing services for the newspaper to an outside entity. If universities opted to print their own newspapers, many institutions would find the initial costs of maintenance and upkeep of printing machinery to be prohibitive. It is also best to choose a printing company that the university has had an established relationship. With the advent of digital cameras and computer software, operation costs have been lower than was printing in the "old days." Online format of student newspapers have also become popular. This format may also drive down cost for student newspapers, but may occupy enormous amounts of space on a university server.

Student Government and Student Organizations

The student government is to represent student interest, provide services to students, and communicate information to students. It is important for student government officials to remember who they represent. It is essential, therefore, for the student government to know the pertinent issues regarding the student body. This can be done through suggestion boxes and student surveys. The student government association represents the student body and can serve as a training ground for those students who wish to go into public services. Officers of the student government association serve as student representatives on university-wide, college-wide, and department-level committees. Some believe that a strong student government association can be troublesome to the campus community because it competes for power with the administration and faculty; however, the relationship between the university president and the student government association does not have to be adversarial. This may be a great opportunity for the university president to mentor and guide a great group of future leaders. I believe that it is important for the student government association to have strong leadership, one that understands the nature of its responsibilities and the importance of working well with the university administration and other constituents. This creates a healthy university and a positive environment. In order to foster a good relationship, the university president should meet with the student government association or the executive cabinet and engage in dialogues about campus improvements and other issues that may arise. Dialogue with the student government also allows the university president to stay informed of pertinent issues that are important to the student body and the university. At Western Illinois University, I speak to the student government association at least once per semester, or at their invitation. Western Illinois University has outstanding student leaders who are professional and take their roles seriously. They engage in the business of the university and are preparing to lead in the global society. These students, most notably, are open to suggestions, willing to look at unconventional solutions to traditional problems, and are mindful of the rules of order when conducting business.

Greek Organizations

There are essentially six types of Greek organizations found on college campuses. Among these organizations are men's fraternities, women's sororities, professional fraternities, honor societies, recognition societies, and service fraternities. For most universities, these organizations can be a source of great energy, pride, and spirit on a campus. In some cases, they can also be a source of great embarrassment. No matter the societal attitudes toward fraternities and sororities, they are a part of the culture and nature of American university life. No matter how we view these organizations, they are big business in our capitalist society. At a number of universities, the social Greek fraternities and sororities have remained segregated; however, there have been individuals who have integrated these organizations throughout the twentieth century. Most social organizations are guided by the National PanHellenic Conference or the National Interfraternity Council.

It is essential that universities build relationships with the national administrative team of any Greek organization that operates on its campus. These national organizations should help to provide oversight to chapters' operation. They should prepare student officers to conduct, operate, and lead the organization's campus chapter. These organizations are voluntary. Membership is a privilege and not a right; therefore, a university does not have the right to force an individual to join or be accepted into a Greek organization. An organization does not have the right to establish a chapter at a university unless it obtains approval from the university. The nature of the relationship between the university and the organization should be defined in advance to distill any future legal issues, if they should arise.

One legal issue that has garnered plenty of attention in recent years is the issue of hazing by fraternities and sororities, and the legal obligation of the university in response to this issue. In March 2003, Walter Dean Jennings III was pledging Psi Epsilon Chi when he was forced to drink numerous pitchers of water to the point of vomiting numerous times. He drank so much water that his brain swelled and he died from water intoxication (Chronicle website, 2007). In 2007, two members of the Florida A&M University chapter of Kappa Alpha Psi Fraternity, Inc., were sentenced to two years in prison for paddling a pledge with wooden canes (Thrash, 2007). In 2012, Yale University became the subject of a federal Title IX investigation after a group of current and former students accused the school of creating a "hostile environment" for women (Inside Higher Ed website, 2012). Central to these allegations was Delta Kappa Epsilon Fraternity, for which pledges marched outside the Yale campus chanting, "No means yes! Yes means anal! (Inside Higher Ed website)." In 2011, a nineteen-year-old sophomore at Cornell University died of alcohol poisoning after allegedly taking part in a Sigma Alpha Epsilon hazing ritual (Winerip, 2012). In response, the student's mother filed a $25 million lawsuit against the fraternity. The individual members of the fraternity who were charged were ultimately found not guilty because of a technicality (Winerip, 2012). In response, Cornell suspended the chapter, and the president of the university directed the college's Greek organizations to end the pledging process, effective fall 2012. Fraternities and sororities must understand that even if they operate houses on campus, this house is on campus and subject to the policies and regulations of the wider university.

I am a member of Alpha Phi Alpha Fraternity, Inc., and I enjoy the social camaraderie and brotherhood that such an organization can bring. I give my undergraduate fraternity brothers a sobering warning. As president of a university, it is my job to do what is in the best interest of the university. I also tell them that if they are caught hazing individuals, do not expect special favors because we are members of the same fraternal organization.

Campus Violence

The shootings at Virginia Tech University, Northern Illinois University, and the University of Alabama at Huntsville campuses received large amounts of media coverage; however, there are several occurrences of campus violence that did not receive widespread media coverage. On the campus of Texas Southern University in 2009, six people, including one student, were shot in a drive-by shooting at a community rally (ABC News website, 2009). In 2007, at Virginia Tech, an undergraduate student killed thirty-two people and wounded seventeen others, and then killed himself on the campus (CNN website, 2013). According to the CNN website timeline (2013) the shooting began around 8:00 A.M. and began to spread among students via text messages. The university president and the leadership team met to decide how to alert the campus around 8:25A.M... Almost an hour-and-a-half would pass before students and staff would be notified. At 9:26 A.M., the university sent its first e-mail warning about the shooting. The university received a call about a shooting on campus in Norris Hall at 9:45 A.M. Virginia Tech officials sent another e-mail to the campus at 9:50 A.M. In the e-mail, everyone was warned to stay inside and away from the windows. At 10:15 A.M., another e-mail was sent notifying everyone that classes were canceled. At 10:52 A.M., university officials sent another e-mail stating the number of people that had been killed and urged everyone to remain inside and for those who had not reached campus to stay away. At 4:30 P.M., the Virginia Tech University President Charles W. Steger and the campus police chief, confirmed that thirty-three people were dead, including the gunman (CNN website, 2013).

In 2008, at Northern Illinois University, a graduate student killed six people and injured twenty-one people before killing himself. Shortly after 3:00 P.M., the gunman walked into a large auditorium where a class was being held and began firing into the crowd of students, killing the instructor (NIU Report, 2008). According to the NIU report, officials alerted students and staff to take cover at 3:30 P.M... At 3:40 pm, the university president and the leadership team canceled classes. At 4:14 P.M., the university reported that the gunman was no longer a threat and urged all students to call their parents and guardians. At 5:15 P.M., a news conference was held to notify the public of the details of the incident.

In 2010, a faculty member at the University of Alabama at Huntsville killed three biology professors and injured three faculty members when she opened fire at a departmental faculty meeting (Brown, 2012). The shooter, who had been denied tenure the previous year, sat quietly at the faculty meeting for about thirty minutes and then began to fire her weapon, starting with those who were closest to her. She then moved around the table shooting her colleagues (Brown, 2012). In 2012, families of those who died filed a wrongful death lawsuit against the shooter and against the University of Alabama at Huntsville (Severson, 2011). In September 2012, the shooter pleaded guilty to one count of capital murder involving two or more people and three counts of attempted murder. She had earlier pleaded not guilty by reason of insanity (Severson, 2011). Due to these shootings, institutions became more aware of campus safety and have implemented various measures to ensure the safety of their campuses.

In the wake of the Virginia Tech shootings, Virginia's governor formed a panel to investigate the shootings (Voice of America website, 2013). There were numerous calls for the dismissal of the university president; however, the governor refused to get involved with the affairs of the university. In 2011, the Department of Education fined the University $55,000 for waiting too long to notify students of the initial shootings (ABC News website, 2012). The fine was the highest amount that the Department of Education could levy for the two violations of the Clery Act of failing to notify students in a timely manner (ABC News website, 2012). In 2012, the parents of two students who were killed filed a wrongful death civil lawsuit. The lawsuit argued that the students' lives could have been saved if school officials had moved more quickly to notify the campus after the first two victims had been shot (ABC News website, 2012).

It is simple to be critical of the handling of the shootings at these two universities, but some valuable lessons were learned from the Virginia Tech situation. It forced universities to develop contingency plans for random violence on their campuses. In fact, the incident at Virginia Tech probably helped the University of Northern Illinois and the University of Alabama at Huntsville to be better prepared for the incidents on their campuses.

Veteran Students

In 1944, President Franklin Delano Roosevelt signed into law what has often been called the most significant piece of legislation ever produced by the U.S. government: the GI Bill of Rights, also known as the Serviceman's Readjustment Act (Cruz, 2008). The original GI Bill guaranteed veterans $300 in pay, financial assistance for higher education and training, weekly unemployment allowance of $20 for fifty-two weeks, and federal guaranteed loans of up to $2,000 (at 4% interest) (Cruz, 2008). The GI Bill helped former servicemen to transition from military service and matriculate to college and move on to productive careers in a wide range of fields. In 2009, the new GI Bill was enacted (US Department of Defense website, 2013). According to the US Department of Defense, the new GI Bill was designed to provide a similar higher education incentive for more than 2 million service members who have served since September 11, 2001. The Post-9/11 GI Bill is designed to cover tuition and fees for in-state public undergraduate higher education for eligible veterans. The Post-9/11 GI Bill also provides a monthly housing stipend and an annual book stipend. In 2010, legislation passed that expanded eligibility for the benefit to an additional 85,000 members of the National Guard and reserves. As the wars in Afghanistan and Iraq end, universities will see an increased number of veterans returning to seek higher education opportunities. Over the next two decades, universities should provide some resources for these veterans' transition back to civilian life as some are dealing with post-traumatic stress disorder and other stress-related illnesses after returning from their tours of duty. Veterans are assets for universities. Veterans can serve as mentors for traditional-age college students and mentor these students on such issues as accountability and responsibility. Veterans can also raise the level of classroom discussions and add to the diversity of the student body.

At Western Illinois University veterans are important to us, and we pride ourselves on being military-friendly. We have been named by G.I. Jobs Magazine for several consecutive years as a military-friendly institution. The U.S. Navy has given permission for Western Illinois University to use the U.S. Marine Corps' official seal, mascot, and nickname, "The Fighting Leathernecks." The use of the Marine Corps' nickname for Western Illinois University's athletic teams (originally the men's teams) was secured by Ray "Rock" Hanson, a former football coach. His love for the Marine Corps and his ties to the military helped him to gain approval for the use of the nickname for WIU's athletic teams. In addition, WIU is the only university that has the distinction of using the Marine Corps' nickname for athletic teams. We have worked hard to make Western Illinois University veteran-friendly. In 2011, Western Illinois University was awarded the Governor's Award for Excellence in Veterans Education, and key personnel have been asked to present best practices as a model program at multiple conferences. Dr. Richard Carter and Western Illinois University were presented with the "Above and Beyond Award" by the Employer Support of the Guard and Reserve.

International Students

Classifying students from other countries has been the subject of debate in the history of American colleges and universities. The term *foreign student is* no longer acceptable, and the acceptable term is "international student." Universities, traditionally, in the United States have taken a "build it and they will come" approach to attracting international students. In 2010, universities with the largest percentage of international undergraduate students in their student bodies included the New School, the Illinois Institute of Technology, the University of Tulsa, the University of Buffalo SUNY, Carnegie Mellon University, and Brandeis University (Hopkins, 2012, US News). In the wake of the tragedies of September 11, 2001, the number of international students enrolled at American colleges and universities declined and then began to rebound about four years later. According to the Institute of International Education, the number of students rose 4.7% to 723,277 during the 2010–2011 academic year (Marklein, USA Today, 2011). As immigration laws were tightened as a response to the calls for tougher national security, the numbers of international students declined. International students and their dependents contributed more than $20 billion to the United States' economy in 2011 (Marklein, USA Today, 2011). There also appears to be an upward trend of international students choosing to study abroad at universities outside of the United States as these numbers increased by almost 4% during the 2009–2010 academic year (Marklein, USA Today, 2011). In 2011, the People's Republic of China was the top country sending students to study in the United States. China sent 157,558 undergraduate and graduate students to study in the United States (Marklein, USA Today, 2011). Other top countries sending students to the United States for study are South Korea, India, Canada, and Taiwan.

The quantity of students is projected to increase to at least 250 million by the year 2025. The vast majority of these students will be international, so with or without massive recruitment efforts a number of international students will enroll at American campuses. At Western Illinois University, we decided to recruit more international students. In 2012, the director of international studies and I traveled to nine countries' embassies in Washington D.C. to promote WIU in hopes of attracting more students to campus. As international students become more visible on campuses, it is imperative that universities prepare local communities that are not familiar with various cultures and ethnicities. These communities must adjust to become more accepting of people who may be different from themselves. Proactive education of the campus and community that focuses on the advantages of diversity will help the adjustment for not only the international students but for the community at-large. It is also good policy to be proactive in countering negative stereotypes associated with international students. The international students' integration into campus and community life is vital to the success of these students. This integration into both will give international students a richer and fuller learning experience inside and outside of the classroom. International student recruitment and retention should be an essential part of any strategic plan and university core values to modernize and globalize the university. Universities must also acknowledge and meet the needs of international students while they are enrolled. If international students do not have meaningful experiences, it will negatively impact the university's international reputation, and agencies and countries will direct their students to other universities.

CHAPTER 7

Admissions and the Administration

The admissions standards for undergraduate and graduate admissions at many institutions should be firmly established collectively through the use of faculty governance. In many cases, faculty committees with input from administrators should develop the criteria that should be used when making admissions decisions on potential students. For most graduate programs, graduate faculty members are involved in the admissions decisions for graduate applicants. Most institutions either use a standard admission or rolling admission to decide students' admittance into the university. In the current educational climate, many institutions are in great competition for students. Students usually apply to several schools, weighing their options and considering numerous factors in making the decision of which university to attend.

A rolling deadline model for admissions is when decisions are made when students have submitted all of the required materials that are needed to make a decision. In the case of rolling admission, students are notified throughout the year of their acceptance status. A rolling admissions process allows students to be notified sooner than a standard admission process. In a rolling process, students should receive their decision within three or four weeks. This allows students to begin the search for financial aid and other scholarships earlier. A quick decision may also aid students in choosing a university.

In general, applications are submitted during the fall semester prior to the academic year in which the applicant is seeking admittance to the college or university. Depending on the guidelines of the institution, deadlines for applications can vary greatly depending on the mission, selectivity, and profile of the institution. In addition, there is usually a fee associated with the applications. The fee is often used to process the applications. A number of universities have begun to utilize electronic admission applications. In this trend, universities believe that a paperless application streamlines procedures, improves accuracy, and reduces the turn-around time on first-time freshman, transfer, and graduate applications. Most colleges do not waive application fees unless an extreme hardship case has been presented.

Admissions Criteria

The criterion for college and university admission in the United States varies greatly, depending on institutional type. Most institutions require all applicants to take a standardized test for admissions consideration. For most American four-year colleges and universities, students are required to take either the ACT (which is a previous abbreviation for American College Testing) or the SAT (which was initially referred to as the Scholastic Achievement Test). Both standardized tests are designed to measure what students know and how well they apply that knowledge. College and university admissions officers use the scores from these tests and other indicators from applicants' academic and extracurricular profiles as predictors for students' success at four-year colleges and universities. At most universities, all students are required to take the SAT or the ACT and have these scores sent to the university of their choice.

In addition to standardized test scores, other primary criteria used in most collegiate admissions decisions are grade point average (GPA), class rank, and relevant high school courses taken. Secondary admissions considerations are extracurricular and co-curricular activities and advanced placement (AP) courses. An increasing trend is to enroll high academically achieving high school students in one or two college-level courses while they complete their high school course work. Students may also be granted credit for AP credit courses taken in high school. If universities are not considering accepting AP credit, the university president and other leaders responsible for admissions can build relationships with school principals and superintendents in order to convey that information. In the end, acceptance of applicants' AP credit may cause students to choose a certain university. Several colleges and universities have recently moved away from requiring undergraduate applicants to submit letters of recommendations; however, in the past, recommendation letters were a large part of undergraduate admissions at many American colleges and universities.

Admission Decisions

Admissions decisions should be made in the Office of Admissions using established criteria. Students should receive an admissions decision soon after all admissions materials are received (i.e., application, test scores, transcripts, etc.) Two to three weeks should be enough time for an admissions committee to make a decision, based on the determined criteria, and notify the applicant. Notifying applicants earlier in the process rather than later has proven to increase institutions' ability to admit more students. For example, Western Illinois University implemented a scholarship program for high-achieving students. The program was designed to notify students early in the admissions process of the amount of funding they will receive based on their standardized test scores and GPA. Presidents and other senior-level administrators should not be involved in making individual decisions on students' admittance to the university. Admissions decisions should be made fairly and impartially, without consideration of any variables other than academic ability, other talents and probability of success. When the criteria for admission are clear, the margin for error when making an admissions decision is generally reduced significantly.

Problems in Admissions

The Office of Admissions is often the portal to the college or university. Although it is not exclusive, the admissions staff is largely responsible for connecting students with the campus community. Admissions counselors are often the first individuals with whom potential students interact. When institutional representatives are not providing accurate, clear, and concise information to potential applicants, it can have a significantly negative impact on campus enrollment. The admissions staff should not mislead students on the availability of academic programs and other services. In addition, when institutions do not have sound enrollment plans that can be executed on an annual basis this may also cause many problems in the admissions area. The function of an admissions office is critical to institutional success.

Depending on the nature of the institutional structure, admissions offices are usually placed in either academic affairs or student affairs. The culture of an institution typically helps the president to decide, along with the administrative leadership team, which division should oversee the daily activities of an admissions or enrollment management staff. Admissions must be able to adapt quickly to changing environments to meet the needs of students who are evolving regularly. The nature of admissions work has changed dramatically in the last twenty-five years. As institutional leaders we must shift to employ best-practices in a timely manner in order to yield the best results. In the past, students applied for admissions on paper and admissions officers relied on students to make applications instead of aggressively recruiting students. The use of technology has changed the landscape of the admissions process.

Using Technology in Admissions

In recent years, the use of technology for recruiting students has increased. Institutions are establishing social media accounts and utilizing podcasts and web-blogs to communicate with and attract more students. Institutional Facebook and Twitter accounts provide information for students, parents, alumni, and friends of the institution. In addition, electronic mail and text messages are increasingly becoming the normal medium for communication among potential students and admissions staff. Admissions staff and others at institutions can use Facebook and other forms of social media to monitor students' activities. In many instances, admissions counselors send text messages to potential students to remind them of important dates, to apprise them of campus activities, and to follow-up with them during the recruitment cycle. At Western Illinois University, many students have commented on how the attention they received through text messaging and other technologies influenced their decisions to attend WIU.

Admissions as Public Relations

As resources diminish, many institutions have adopted policies that allow students who are residents of neighboring states to receive in-state tuition. When tuition reciprocity agreements were implemented years ago, the offer was typically extended only to students who lived in boarding counties in other states; however, the current educational and economic climate has served as a catalyst for allowing students in neighboring states to attend and pay in-state tuition, regardless of their originating county. This strategy was implemented to increase our competitiveness and make the institution more marketable. Western Illinois University offers in-state tuition to all students who live in states that have a land border with Illinois, with the exception being Kentucky; therefore, students who are permanent residents of Indiana, Iowa, Missouri, and Wisconsin can receive in-state tuition at Western Illinois University. Although Illinois has water border with Michigan, students who are permanent residents of Michigan do not receive in-state tuition at WIU.

In addition, alumni and friends of the institution can provide support. The president generally seeks to maintain or establish positive working relationships with alumni and friends of the institution. The individual responsible for alumni affairs programs typically helps the president to cultivate these relationships. It is imperative that the president preserves and protects the institutions' brand and reputation. Positive public relations will help institutions expand their endowments and other contributions, and it will increase an institution's ability to provide much needed funding and scholarships for students during uncertain economic times.

Educational Opportunities for Marginal Students

There are students who are not properly prepared for the rigors of college. Some students are not ready to adjust to the norms, customs, and cultures of academic environments. All students are not suited to attend four-year institutions. When underprepared students apply to institutions, what should we do with the applications of these students? At many public, comprehensive, regional institutions, higher education is about opportunity. Some marginal students who show potential of success should be admitted and have the opportunity to succeed; however, I do understand that some students who desire admission to a university are underprepared. For these students, conditional admission should be utilized.

Conditional, provisional, or alternative admissions refers to a student who is admitted to an institution on the condition that he or she meet some criteria such as completion of remedial courses or achievement of a set grade point average (usually a "C" or better), and limited credit hour enrollment. After successfully meeting the set conditions, conditional status is usually removed. Some institutions have ceased using "conditional admission," whereas others have still used it but do not publicize it as an option for admission. Conditional admission allows students to enter a college or university to provide evidence that they can excel at collegiate-level work. It places the burden of proof solely on the student, and most motivated students are able to meet this challenge and succeed. At a time when colleges and universities are competing for students while becoming more accountable for retention and graduation rates, some institutions view conditionally admitted students who have been deemed "at-risk" a significant liability. Conditional admission is a form of great opportunity for at-risk, first-generation, and underprepared students.

Transfer Students

Due to the rising costs of tuition and fees at four-year universities, many students are choosing to begin their higher education at two-year colleges. Transfer students are therefore becoming a large portion of the student population for many four-year colleges and universities. Many academic leaders at two- and four-year institutions are working collaboratively and creatively to establish seamless pipelines for students to transfer to the four-year institutions to earn their baccalaureate degrees. These 2+2 programs and other articulation agreements help to provide transfer students with clear guides to completing a baccalaureate degree upon earning their associate degrees at two-year colleges.

Western Illinois University takes great pride in being a transfer-friendly institution. WIU has articulation agreements with several two-year institutions in Illinois and with some two-year institutions in other states. The president signs institutional agreements and works with the provost's office to provide support and publicity for these academic agreements that attract students to the university. Transfer students often have different needs than do native students. As president, therefore, it is imperative that I provide support to various entities within academic affairs and student services to ensure that transfer students' needs are being addressed. Institutions must have a culture of student support, particularly when students must navigate a new educational environment after having been in college at another institution.

The admissions area is a very crucial and vital part of a thriving institution and its sustainability. Most states' funding formulas are appropriated based on student enrollment. Although the competition to recruit and retain students has increased in recent years, it is imperative that institutions maintain quality when admitting students. The admissions standards for undergraduate and graduate admissions should not be diminished for the sake of increasing numbers. Admitting students for the sake of increasing numbers may be beneficial in the short term, but it may negatively impact retention and graduation rates.

CHAPTER 8

Intercollegiate Athletics and the University Presidency

Intercollegiate sports are competitions between two colleges or institutions of higher learning. The United States is fascinated with collegiate sports. In fact, I believe that college football and basketball have surpassed baseball as America's pastime. I am a former athlete. I was a track and cross-country athlete as an undergraduate at Tuskegee University. When I transferred to Alabama A&M University, I continued to run track on the collegiate level. During my tenure at the University of Maryland Eastern Shore, I also served as an assistant track coach. Collegiate sports have grown since they began with a rowing competition between Harvard University and Yale University in 1852 (Smith, 1988). A few years later, Amherst University and Williams College held the first intercollegiate baseball competition in 1859 (Smith, 2011). The first intercollegiate football competition took place when Rutgers University took on Princeton University in 1869 (Smith, 2011).

Collegiate sports at American universities have become a part of the higher education social fabric. The National Collegiate Athletic Association (NCAA) and the National Association of Intercollegiate Athletics are the two governing bodies that provide oversight of intercollegiate sports and universities. Most colleges have joined athletic conferences, and these conferences also provide oversight for the universities. Intercollegiate sports and universities have become big business and quite profitable for conferences. In 2010, two of the most profitable college athletic conferences were the Southeastern Conference (SEC), which earned more than $1 billion, and the Big Ten Conference (Big 10), which earned more than $905 million (Branch, 2011). It is a different story when it comes to athletic conferences that sponsor historically black colleges and universities and other small, predominantly white institutions. These smaller conferences do not generate the kinds of dollars that the Big 10 and SEC conferences generate because they do not have large student enrollments, large stadiums, lucrative television contracts, sponsorships by large corporations, and other large revenue streams for licensed apparel.

Total Revenues without Expenses for HBCU Affiliated Conferences	
Mid-Eastern Athletic Conference	$105,524,230
Southwestern Athletic Conference	$67,642,243
Central Intercollegiate Athletic Association	$38,157,559
Southern Intercollegiate Athletic Conference	$27,284,256
Gulf Coast Athletic Conference	$22,660,011

Source: U.S. Department of Education 2010

Universities have embraced athletic conference affiliation. The more afflu-ent conferences have advanced. The university president must be concerned by the high price tag of collegiate athletics. In 2009, the Knight Commission re-leased a report that stated that college presidents believed that the skyrocketing costs of collegiate athletics could not be sustained. University presidents from Football Bowl Series institutions reported that the cost associated with their ath-letic budgets were increasing faster than their academic budgets. The Knight Report (2009) specifically revealed the six following key findings:

1. Dilemma of reform—Although university presidents recognize the need for reform, there is a lack of clear consensus about the best way to affect change. Nearly three-quarters believe that athletics present more unique challenges than other areas of the university regarding cost control. A majority believe institutions must act collectively to address these esca-lating costs.

2. Sustainability—Less than one-quarter of presidents believe intercol-legiate athletics are sustainable in their current form at FBS institutions nationally. Two-thirds view their own programs as sustainable; but nearly half (48%) express concern that the current economic outlook will affect the number of varsity sports their institution can support in the future.

3. Salaries—When asked about salaries across FBS institutions nationally, an overwhelming majority (85%) of FBS university presidents indicate they feel compensation is excessive for football and basketball coaches. Viewed as the greatest impediment to sustainability, coaches' salaries are costs that are difficult to control.

4. Growing Divide between Haves and Have-Nots—A major concern is the growing imbalance between financially strong and weak programs. Presidents of less-competitive institutions feel that their programs are unfairly exploited.

5. Transparency—More than 80% of presidents believe greater financial transparency is needed.
6. Benefits of Athletics—College presidents perceive athletic success provides substantial benefits to the institution, such as generating higher levels of fundraising, attracting better-qualified students, enhancing school spirit, and raising the profile of the institution. Although empirical research generally does not support a significant correlation between athletic success and increased donations or student quality, FBS university presidents are swayed by personal experience that there are cross-institutional benefits of a winning sports program.

College athletics are a big enterprise, and the financial pressures on small universities are constant. For some universities that have the assistance of large television contracts, big name coaches, and large gate receipts, college sports are seemingly as important as academics. Collegiate sports fall within the broad educational, social, and physical values in sports. College sports are unfortunately followed so closely that a college team's win–loss records have become a symbol of the success and failure of an institution. It is sad that some students are basing their decision on what college to attend on the success and failure of sports programs. When the University of Florida's basketball and football teams won national championships in 2006, the number of applications for admission increased significantly. If student admission applications increase, other factors usually increase, including SAT scores, GPAs, and diversity; however so does the costs of operating athletic programs.

A recent trend at universities is to raise student fees to support university athletics, which can range from $30 per year to more than $1,000. In most cases, fee increases must be voted on and approved by students. In some cases, this means that students are lobbied like private donors to the benefits of sports programs at the university. Recently, fee increases have been voted down at Fresno State University, Long Beach State University, and the University of New Orleans. In the case of Fresno State, the university overrode the vote and increased the student fees to start two women's sports programs. At North Texas University and Utah State University, students voted to raise fees to support their athletic programs. Recent trends show that subsidies to college athletic programs have equaled or surpassed funding to university libraries at numerous universities.

Title IX and the University

College athletics for women have steadily advanced since the enactment of Title IX of the Education Amendments of 1972. Title IX is the federal civil rights law that prohibits sex discrimination in education and is a key reason for the rise of intercollegiate athletics for women. As the result of Title IX, universities had to invest in women sports programs and begin to distribute dollars to women's athletic programs. Section 20 of the law specifically states:

> No person in the United States shall, on the basis of sex, be excluded from participation in, be denied the benefits of, or be subjected to discrimination under any education program or activity receiving federal financial assistance...

In 1975, the final clause of Title IX was signed into law and included provisions prohibiting sex discrimination in athletics. The regulations pertaining to athletics require that an institution that sponsors interscholastic, intercollegiate, club, or intramural athletics shall provide "equal athletic opportunity" for male and female athletes. Since the passing of Title IX, some universities have continued to struggle with balancing the offerings of women's and men's sports programs. In successfully complying with Title IX requirements, NCAA institutions must meet one of the requirements in the "three prong test" as follows:

1. Prong one—Provide athletic participation opportunities that are substantially proportionate to student enrollment. This part of the test is satisfied when participation opportunities for men and women are "substantially proportionate" to their respective undergraduate enrollment.
2. Prong two—Demonstrate a continual expansion of athletic opportunities for the underrepresented sex. This part of the test is satisfied when an institution has a history and continuing practice of program expansion that is responsive to the developing interests and abilities of the underrepresented sex (typically female).
3. Prong three—Full and effective accommodation of the interest and ability of underrepresented sex. This part of the test is satisfied when an institution is meeting the interests and abilities of its female students, even where there are disproportionately fewer females than males participating in sports.

In 2010, women comprised the majority of students in many small liberal arts colleges as well as larger public and private schools, such as Oberlin College (55%), the University of Georgia (58%), and New York University (61%) (Rose, 2010). According to the National Center for Education Statistics, women constituted approximately 57% of students enrolled in American colleges and universities during the 2012–2013 academic year. With these numbers, one can see that universities must provide equal opportunities for women. At most of institutions of higher learning women outnumber men. The increase of women on college campuses has increased because of Title IX since the 1970s. Some schools have struggled to remain Title IX compliant in athletics. As sports programs continue to become Title IX–compliant, some trends are emerging. One is that schools that sponsor football find it difficult to remain complaint and offer equal opportunities for women athletes. Smaller schools also find it less difficult than do large universities to comply with Title IX. It also appears that a university's reputation and its commitment to goals of academic integrity, cultural diversity, and racial diversity show that there may be a greater eagerness toward creating equality in their sports programs.

The university president is the chief executive officer of the university. The president is praised with the success of programs both academic and athletic. Likewise, the university president is blamed when programs fail. The university must stay well-informed about athletic polices. Sports programs are highly visible to the public, and the public will probably follow the athletic program more closely than any other program at the university. Sports columns and score reports in the media can be a weekly advertisement for a university or a public relations nightmare. In this light, university presidents, need to pay close attention to sports and have a close relationship with the faculty athletic committee and the athletic director. The university president should also keep the board of trustees informed of the developments of athletics. Sound objectives and well-defined policies governing athletics at a university will assist in curtailing some problems. The pressures to win may contribute to "cutting corners" and not following NCAA polices, and so on. University presidents must resist this kind of temptation.

The lure of big-time football is all the rage at a few universities. There is evidence of this by the mere fact that many universities are moving to college football's top level. Football Bowl Series (FBS) gives schools a chance at what some are calling the "Doug Flutie Effect." The name is a reference to the impact the success of quarterback Doug Flutie had on the image and reputation of

Boston College. Flutie, who won the Heisman Trophy in 1984, was successful on the football field, and this exposure helped to rebrand the institution and enhance its image and reputation. Flutie's heroics on the gridiron, particularly the memorable "Hail Mary pass" that led to an upset of the University of Miami Hurricanes, who were a national powerhouse in football, were key to enhancing Boston College's athletics program. Prior to Flutie's coming on the scene, Boston College was a regional school and its student body was predominantly comprised of Catholic students from the East Coast. The exposure gained via Flutie and the football program made the university a national school and expanded the institution's reach and improved its image overnight. It is important to note that Boston College had the infrastructure in place to accommodate its new-found popularity and status. Many smaller schools do not have the infrastructure in place to go from a regional to national university so quickly. To move up in status of football and all sports is ultimately a business decision, and the university president and the leadership team must conduct a cost–benefit analysis and ponder a number of questions. Central questions to be examined before deciding to pursue big-time athletics are:

1. What will be the return on investment if the university moves to big-time athletics?
2. Will a move to big-time athletics increase the exposure to offset the costs in the annual budget?
3. Will a move to big time athletics attract a significantly higher caliber of students and faculty?
4. Will a move to big-time athletics translate to increased giving from existing donors and alumni?

The university president should lead these discussions. Coaches' salaries at big-time sports programs have grown exponentially over the years. According to figures released by the *USA Today,* football coaches were compensated $1.47 million on average in 2011. This increase has occurred as most public universities have had major cuts in state funding. Since 2006, the average pay for college football coaches grew 55% to $950,000. According to the *USA Today* college football salary data base in 2006–2011, all head football coaches in the FBS division earned a six-figure salary or above, and most of these coaches had multimillion dollar contracts that could be supplemented by bonus monies

Highest Paid College Football Coaches in 2011	
Mack Brown, University of Texas	$5,193,500
Nick Saban, University of Alabama	$4,833, 333
Bob Stoops, University of Oklahoma	$4,075,000
Les Miles, Louisiana State University	$3,856,417
Kirk Ferentz, University of Iowa	$3,785,000
Bobby Petrino, University of Arkansas	$3,638,000
Gene Chizik, Auburn University	$3,500,000
Brady Hoke, University of Michigan	$3,254,000

Source: USA Today college football salary data base in 2006–2011

Similar to the football salaries, according to the *USA Today*, college basketball coaches' salaries for 2011–2012 were also high. Most head basketball coaches in the NCAA tournament earned a six-figure salary or above, and most of these coaches had multimillion dollar contracts that could be supplemented by bonus monies. The exception was the head basketball coach for Mississippi Valley State University, whose salary was $87,500 with a bonus of $7,292.

Highest Paid College Basketball Coaches Salaries 2012	
John Calipari, University of Kentucky	$4,000,000
Tom Izzo, Michigan State University	$3,500,000
Billy Donovan, University of Florida	$3,500,000
Bill Self, University of Kansas	$3,000,000
Rick Pitino, University of Louisville	$2,500,000
Thad Matta, Ohio State University	$2,500,000
Rick Barnes, University of Texas	$2,400,000
Mike Krzyzewski, Duke University	$2,400,000

Source: Forbes Magazine

Intercollegiate athletics is a large portion of the American collegiate experience. Some colleges and universities are more recognized for their athletics programs rather than for their academic programs. American culture has emphasized an importance on collegiate sports and the competitive spirit that athletics promotes. Collegiate programs have grown significantly since the mid-nineteenth century. Athletics are an important part of students' extracurricular activities and can foster a great sense of school spirit and pride. Many alumni are interested in the success of the athletic programs at their alma mater and are more likely to attend sporting events to provide their support for the institution. In addition, sporting events can be used as a recruiting tool to showcase an institution. Athletics is a catalyst that often serves as an advertisement to encourage individuals to take an in-depth look at the institution.

CHAPTER 9

Religion, Diversity, and the University Presidency

There are various forms of discrimination on university and college campuses in the United States. Sexism and racism combined with religious dogma and homophobia can make for a volatile mix when college-aged individuals begin to discuss these issues. It has been widely thought that secular American universities are a bastion of atheism divorced from religious thought unless it is a purely academic study of religion or the bible as literature. Most universities, especially those who have their foundations set in the religious tradition, are linked to organized religion. In 1636, Harvard University aimed to educate an illiterate white male clergy. In Harvard's early years, most of its classes were devoted to the ministry, and most of the institution's presidents were ministers (Thelin, 2011). In 1948, Brandies University was started by the Jewish community to combat anti-Semitism (Thelin, 2011). Although Brandies' mission has expanded, most of its students continue to be Jewish. Most of the private historically black colleges and universities were formed by denominational religious organizations or philanthropic organizations to train clergy and to educate the black race, which had been recently freed from slavery just after the Civil War. There are a number of universities that were started and continue to hold religious affiliations. The University of Notre Dame, Xavier University of Louisiana, and Boston College hold to their Catholic founding. Brigham Young University holds to its Church of Latter Day Saints' affiliation. Stillman College and Monmouth College hold to their Presbyterian founding. Baylor University, Shaw University, and Morehouse College continue to hold to their Baptist traditions.

Many of these universities have broken formal ties with religious denominations. In fact, on some campuses, the only evidence that one will see of this partnership is the gothic style architecture of some of the campus buildings or the college chapel that is used for some of the universities' ceremonies. During the 1960s, organized religion and religious activities declined on college campuses. In fact, some religious conservatives and conservative politicians have claimed that academia is endorsing atheism at American universities.

Religious Organization and Programs

In the past, the issue of religion has been a somewhat monolithic issue with most religious organizations being Protestant on American college campuses. To avoid any controversies at state-supported public universities, most administrators and university presidents have taken a hands-off approach to religion on campus and have not promoted one religious group over another. As the United State has become more religiously diverse, it has forced university administrations not to hide behind this hands-off approach as invitations from various religious organizations are extended to the university president. When scheduling permits, the university president should attend events when an invitation is extended without the endorsement of the religion. The separation of church and state exists. I identify as Protestant, and I proclaim Christianity as my faith; however, I am sophisticated enough in my faith to recognize other faiths. University presidents must remember that it is our duty to represent all that are affiliated with the university regardless of their background. At most private historically black colleges, a chapel on campus was a common fixture. The chapel served as a place and a platform for African American leaders to discuss social, political, and cultural issues. In fact, it was in the chapel at Morehouse College that Martin Luther King, Jr., first became influenced by Morehouse President Benjamin E. Mays. There are similar stories at historically black colleges throughout the nation. The Rankin Chapel at Howard University, the Woodworth Chapel at Tougaloo College, Sisters Chapel at Spelman College, and Allen Chapel at Paul Quinn College are campus centers for spiritual enlightenment, community activism, and political mobilization.

Religious Organizations and University Policies

Recently, several religious organizations have experienced policy conflicts at their universities. According to FIRE which is a nonprofit educational foundation that unites civil rights and civil liberties leaders, scholars, journalists, and public intellectuals, Muslim students faced discrimination. In 2003, the Muslim Students Association (MSA) of Louisiana State University was informed that a new policy requiring all groups explicitly to state that they would not deny membership on the basis of a list of criteria including "religion" and "sexual orientation" was implemented (French, 2005). The MSA felt that the language was not consistent with their religious beliefs and the mission of their organization; therefore, they refused to include the required language in their organization's constitution. As a result of this decision, MSA was denied recognition by the university's administration and the group was stripped of all privileges to use on-campus facilities, distribute literature, and other activities on campus. These are benefits and privileges that are offered to student groups. One year later, Louisiana State University reversed its decision and granted official recognition to the MSA.

In 2005, the University of California's Hasting Law School refused to recognize the Christian Legal Society as a campus organization (*Christian Legal Society v. Martinez*, 2010). In 2010, the group filed a lawsuit but the United States Supreme Court ruled in favor to the university's decision not to grant the group recognition unless its leadership would be accessible to all people regardless of their religion (*Christian Legal Society v. Martinez*, 2010). Since this ruling, Christian and other religious clubs have been challenged at other universities based on the same rationale. A rash of universities since then have considered or adopted all-comers policies that have threatened the status of religious student organizations.

In August, 2011, several Christian student groups applied to receive recognized status at San Diego State University and they were denied (Choate Neilson, 2012). The groups filed a lawsuit arguing that their First Amendment rights had been denied. The district court disagreed and the court of appeals upheld the decision (*Alpha Delta Chi-Delta Chapter v. Charles Reed*, 2011). In 2012, Vanderbilt University was involved in a case that has received considerable attention. Vanderbilt University adopted a policy where leadership in religious organizations must be open to all individuals whether or not these individuals subscribe to the practices of the religion. The religious groups at Vanderbilt are open to all individuals, but they believe that their leadership should be reserved for those who practice the group's beliefs. Vanderbilt stated that religious groups are free to choose their leaders but must allow any student to be a member and to run for office, regardless of their beliefs. Religious discrimination is wrong. Our country was founded on religious freedom, and our universities should embrace this principle.

Racism on Campus

Students and faculty alike continue to struggle with the issue of racism on college campuses. During the 1960s, there was a movement to start Black Studies programs on many college campuses. This call for Black Studies led to protests on predominately white campuses and historically black colleges. There were some schools, particularly those in the South, which held to the traditions and customs of segregation from the past. Southern states resisted acceptance of the United States Supreme Court decision of *Brown v. Board of Education* (1954), which called for the integration of all public schools. Although this mandate

was primarily aimed at K–12 public schools, many universities would not comply with the ruling. For example, Bob Jones University did not admit African
American students until the 1970s. Even though the institution slowly began to
admit non–white students in the 1970s, the institution's policies included a ban
on interracial dating (Firmin & Firebaugh, 2008). In 1998, a public relations
spokesman for the university explained the school's prohibition against interracial dating, "God has separated people for his own purposes. He has erected
barriers between the nations, not only land and sea barriers, but also ethnic, cultural, and language barriers. God has made people different from one another
and intends those differences to remain. Bob Jones University is opposed to in-
termarriage of the races because it breaks down the barriers God has established
(Firmin & Firebaugh, 2008). Bob Jones University did not officially end its ban
against interracial dating until 2000 (Firmin & Firebaugh, 2008).

In 2003, Brown University President Ruth Simmons apologized for the
university's use of slave labor in constructing its buildings on campus (Wilder,
2013). Dr. Simmons also convened a campus wide committee to study the use of
slave labor at the university. The University Steering Committee on Slavery and
Justice released a 100-page report on the university's use of slave labor and its
participation in the transatlantic slave trade. When discussing her reasoning for
convening this committee, Dr. Simmons stated:

> This is an effort designed to involve the campus community in a dis-
> covery of our past... Understanding our history and suggesting how the
> full truth of that history can be incorporated into our common traditions
> will not be easy. But, then, it doesn't have to be (Wilder, 2003).

In 2004, the faculty senate at the University of Alabama issued a formal
apology to the descendants of slaves who were owned by faculty members or
who worked on campus during the antebellum period (Clark & Fine, 2010). The
action was met on campus both with praise and complaints that it was pointless
for anyone to apologize for the sins of the 1800s (Clark & Fine, 2010). Even
in the twenty-first century, there continues to be evidence of racism on college
campuses. There have reportedly been instances of nooses placed on the following campuses since 2000: University of Maryland, California State University at
Fullerton, Purdue University, and Columbia University. Nooses are historically
an age-old symbol of racial intimidation. Other racist evidence on college campuses includes "Crossing the Border" parties, "Ghetto" parties, "Food Stamp"

parties in which white students wear blackface, crawl under barbed-wire fences, or use food stamps as tender to gain admission into the party. A public outcry on this did not occur until images of these events were posted on social media.

In 2011, a Murray State University professor resigned after referring to slavery while making a point about two African American students being late to a class allegedly telling that "tardiness" was a part of their heritage and "the slaves never showed up on time, so their owners often lashed them for it (Schreiner, 2011). Also in 2011, at the University of Alabama, a white student was accused of yelling a racial slur from his fraternity house at a black student (Grasgreen, 2011). The school did not reveal the student's punishment, and the national president of the fraternity apologized personally to the African American student. Less than a week later at the university, racial and ethnic epithets were written on three sidewalks near a central and well-traveled campus green area.

Although the preceding examples were blatant cases of racism on college campuses, there are still subtle forms of racism on American college and university campuses as there are in American society. When I travel wearing Western Illinois University paraphernalia, I am invariably asked if I am an athletic coach or recruiter of some sort. For some people, the stereotype of a university president is a silver-haired white male. It is true that white male presidents comprise a majority at predominantly white colleges and universities. However, the number of African Americans becoming presidents at those colleges and universities, though still low, is slowly increasing. Some examples include Shirley Ann Jackson at Rensselaer Polytechnic Institute, Lee Pelton at Emerson College, Freeman Hrabowski at the University of Maryland Baltimore County, Roderick McDavis at Ohio University, Ronald Crutcher at Wheaton College, Michael Drake, the Ohio State University, Elson Floyd, Washington State University, Rodney Bennett, University of Southern Mississippi, and Chris Howard at Hampden-Sydney College. It is still difficult for some people to believe that an African American male wearing a university affiliated golf shirt is not an athletic coach or recruiter. It is even more difficult for these individuals to believe that African Americans hold the position of university president at predominantly white institutions in this country. Is this racism or a simple mistake on their behalf? I do not know. It is an issue that people must address individually and universities must tackle as a whole.

Sexism on Campus

Sexism is discrimination based on one's sex. Sexism is typically defined as limiting women's roles in society based on their gender. It is the discrimination or devaluation based on a person's sex. For example, people may be restricted to certain job opportunities based on sex. Sexist behavior can appear in the classroom in the form of language. When professors always use the gender pronoun "he," it can be perceived as sexist. When possible, faculty should attempt to use gender-neutral language, and faculty should never use sexist jokes to make points in class or in class discussions in general. There can be erroneous assumptions made about women, especially when it is assumed that females do not have interests and abilities that are typically relegated to men. One erroneous assumption is that females are not good at math and science.

These assumptions can allow faculty members to possess lower expectations for women. Sexism can occur when letters of recommendations are written for female students. In recommendation letters, women candidates are described as agreeable and helpful, which may suggest that these women may not be leaders. Male candidates may be described as aggressive, innovative, and confident, which are descriptors for future leaders.

In addition, women may not be considered for chairperson, dean, and provost positions because these positions may be seen as men's jobs. Many of the duties and the activities associated with these positions could be interpreted as stereotypically male. For example, many of the preferred qualifications in the following advertisements for a university president and for a provost and vice president may be interpreted as stereotypical male characteristics.

Preferred Qualifications

In its search, the College will assess the candidate's leadership and ability to:

- Demonstrate proficiency in oral and written communications and interpersonal skills.
- Develop and articulate a vision for the future of the College.
- Maintain a system of long- and short-range planning that provides for future educational programs, financial resources, facilities, and student services.
- Demonstrate a record of successful program development and evaluation.
- Demonstrate a record of successful administration of finances, budget, facilities, and personnel.
- Develop successful alliances with various organizations, including strengthening partnerships with public schools, community groups, governmental agencies, and local business and industry.

- Demonstrate participation on behalf of economic development and business/industry recruitment efforts, and value the importance of industry training and workforce development to the community.
- Participate visibly in public relations, resource development, and fundraising for the College.
- Demonstrate strong leadership in service to the local community.

Many of the duties in the advertisement are stereotypically associated with the knowledge, skills, and abilities of men and leadership in the academia. The following is an advertisement for a provost and vice president position is stereotypically masculine in its descriptors.

The successful candidate will:

- Be a robust and resilient advocate for the Academic mission of the University.
- Build community, cooperation, and collegiality among administration, faculty, staff and students.
- Be a model of scholarly excellence and have a sustained career of publication.
- Respect faculty governance as well as the intellectual and ethical standards of the profession.
- Be an effective steward of our academic reputation as we move toward national prominence.
- Approach contemporary issues in higher education with innovation and creativity.
- Inspire both independence as well as a common vision among its liberal arts and professional colleges.
- Be devoted to existing initiatives and future projects that strengthen diversity.
- Have an earned doctorate and a record of achievement in teaching and scholarship commensurate with appointment as a tenured professor in a discipline offered at the university.

In order to have a more balanced campus community based on gender, university presidents should work with the diversity officer, equal opportunity and access, or the human resources office on campus to insure that hiring practices are equitable. In addition, there should be programs that enhance the hiring of people who are underrepresented in certain areas. When applicable, advertising for campus positions should be broad and target audiences that may not otherwise apply for presidencies or other leadership positions. Women in senior leadership positions serve as examples for other women who may aspire to be in leadership positions.

GBLT on Campus

In 1969, at the Stonewall Inn in Greenwich Village, New York, gay members of the community participated in a series of violent demonstrations against the city police (Wright, 1999). The New York Police Department began a crackdown of establishments that catered to the gay community (Wright, 1999). As a result of the violence and the crackdown, gay people organized and began to protest and organize an activist group. This incident at Stonewall Inn and the subsequent activities that followed were the beginning of educating the masses in America about gays and lesbians.

College is about learning and learning about other cultures, religions, and lifestyles. Learning about these differences is essential to being a full functioning individual in a free society. On many college and university campuses, safe spaces have been established. Safe spaces are places where gay and lesbian students can feel safe discussing their experiences with faculty and staff members. Maryland's Bowie State University opened a Lesbian, Gay, Bisexual, Transgender, Queer, Intersexed, and Allies Resource Center (Martin-National Public Radio, 2012). The rationale in creating such a center lies in the belief that there are special places set aside for students of particular backgrounds, especially members of minority groups and gays and lesbians should have the same privilege as these other groups (Martin-National Public Radio, 2012). Bowie State is believed to be the first historically black college or university to open this kind of resource center, according to the GBLT advocacy group human rights campaign (Martin-National Public Radio, 2012). Advocates believe that such a resource center is needed to address issues of homophobia on campus and to serve as place where students can find articles, books, and programs on gay and lesbian culture. The center can also be a resource for explaining misconceptions about the openness to the broader communities.

CHAPTER 10

University Presidency, Leadership, and Legacy

Fishbowl Effect

The fishbowl effect is the hyperscrutiny that all public figures face in their daily lives. All public figures are under scrutiny, and the university president is not an exception. As a university president, one has to expect the attention that comes with the title. The public sometimes places unrealistic expectations on presidents and does not recognize that they are human beings like everyone else. For example, the public can be critical over the most unimportant things, such as the color of my tie, whether my shoes match my belt, if I am clean shaven, and even what brand of suit I wear. A university president must be strong and be able to accept valid and invalid criticism. This means being able to deal with the overindulgent critics who take aim at individuals both professionally and personally. The fishbowl effect can also have a significant impact on the president's family. A president's spouse and children can also unfortunately be subject to scrutiny, and a president must be aware of this and protect them at all costs.

University presidents, as most public figures, are held to a higher standard than most individuals. I am cognizant of everything that I say and do in in the public eye. For the university president, the fishbowl effect is a reality. For a university president, there is no such thing as a private life. I am reminded of a time when I had rushed into a local store and realized that I had on knee-length casual shorts because I did not have time to change my clothing. I noticed individuals whom I recognized from the university and I was trying to avoid them because I was uncomfortable with my attire. I simply wanted to purchase the items that I had gathered quickly and leave before anyone noticed me or the attire that I was wearing. Later that day, a student mentioned that I was in the local store because he had seen my picture on twitter. To my surprise, apparently, someone had taken a picture of me and placed it on twitter. As a university president, every move you make is observed, noted, scrutinized, and filed away for others to be judged against the behavior of past presidents and presidents at other universities.

Family Time

I pride myself in being a family man. I am committed to being the best husband and father that I can be. Although my schedule is typically filled with events and meetings, I insist on scheduling family time. My family is important to me. They will always come first and they are aware that I will be there if they need me. In many instances, I plan my schedule around their events and cancel appointments, if need be, because it is important that I am always there.

For example, both of my sons are track athletes, and I make sure to attend many of their track meets. This is no different than the way things were before I became a president. I always found the time to balance my family life and my career even as an up and coming professional. I have been married for twenty-seven years, and I still date my wife. We try to go to dinner and catch a movie every now and then. I talk to her about our children, our extended families, and current events. I make it point not to discuss university business with my wife. That is our time and we all respect that.

Personal Time

My alarm goes off every morning at 4:50 A.M. It is important that I start my day with a daily devotion and then do my morning workout. I have a regular exercise routine that involves running, push-ups, abdominal exercises, weightlifting, and stretching. These exercises allow me to stay healthy and to get my body and soul prepared for the activities and challenges of the day. My workout routine helps me to deal with issues effectively and helps to ward off stress. I use my personal time to reflect and handle personal business. I get an annual physical, and I make sure that I eat properly and get the proper amount of sleep. This helps me to clear my mind and focus on the pertinent issues. I also meditate and take long walks that allow me to unwind. Individuals often tell me that I manage stress well, and I handle issues calmly. I like nature. When I go to my childhood home in Alabama I like to take long walks across the home farm. This allows me to reminisce on my past experiences, and to think about my travels and journey to the presidency. It also gives me the opportunity to think about my humble beginnings and the tasks that are before me. It is imperative to have personal time to help balance the total individual.

Search Process and Salary

Recent trends indicate that colleges and universities hire consulting firms to conduct their presidential searches. In the search process for a university president, there is a call for nominations and applications which includes a position description. Typically, the announcement indicates that applicants can submit materials for the presidency by a specified deadline. Similarly, persons may nominate individuals who they believe are qualified for the presidency. These firms often present names of candidates whose credentials, experience, and expertise may be congruent with the institutions' missions and current state. Additionally, the consulting firms conduct a vetting process. In this process, a candidate's experience, background, credentials, awards, and other information provided in the application is verified. Further, the vetting process may include gathering intelligence on a broader perspective of a candidate's personal and professional history. Depending on the request of the hiring authority, the firm presents the information regarding each candidate and a decision to interview a certain number of candidates is made. Normally, initial candidates are interviewed at off-campus locations to ensure confidentiality and the search committee normally signs a confidentiality agreement. The next step in the process typically involves an on-campus interview for each finalist. This is when candidates meet with students, faculty, staff, administrators, and the community.

When I was a presidential candidate in search processes, I interviewed with all constituencies fielding questions and making formal presentations. During these meetings, I shared my vision and my plans and goals for those institutions if I were selected. It was important for me to share my knowledge and my understanding of current challenges and trends in higher education. Also, I shared my leadership style and how I would manage the social, political and administrative culture of the institution. Though this process may vary at different institutions, it is important that presidential candidates be confident and has knowledge of that particular institution. When preparing for each interview, I make sure that I research the institutions' history, current status, and learn pertinent information about individuals with who I may be meeting. After completing the campus interviews, individuals must wait to see if a presidency will be offered. After an offer is received, contract and salary negotiations begin.

While a university president's salary tends to be high, an individual takes a great risk in accepting the president's position. Most candidates are well established in current positions and communities with long term benefits and retirement plans in place. Although some university presidents live in a residence provided by the institution, many of them have great difficulty selling their personal homes or take a major financial loss in the move. While all new presidents hope for a long and rewarding career at the new institution, there are many factors beyond the control of the president that may create an uncertain future. In addition, because of the budget difficulties in many states, presidents often defer their pay increases or simply donate the increases to scholarship funds. For these reasons, it is important that a new university president negotiates a fair compensation package that results in a salary that reflects the status of the position and the risks associated with leadership. There is a wide range of compensation for a university president. The size, financial health, and status of the university generally determine the salary.

In negotiating salaries and compensation packages, some presidents hire attorneys or agents to negotiate on their behalf, while others engage in this process directly. In my contemplation of a salary offer, I benchmarked the salaries of presidents at similar institutions and my predecessor to determine if the offer was acceptable to me and my family. I also consulted with mentors, sitting presidents, and others. While contract negotiation and acceptance of the presidency bring the search process to a close, it is the official beginning of the relationship with an institution and then the real work begins. Below are examples of a few of the highest paid presidents in the country.

Highest Paid Public College Presidents in 2013	
E. Gordon Gee, Ohio State University	$6,057,615
R. Bowen Loftin, Texas A&M University at College Station	$1,636,274
Hamid A. Shirvani, North Dakota University System	$1,311,095
Michael F. Adams, University of Georgia	$1,295,954
Renu Khator, University of Houston (Main Campus)	$1,266,000
Sally K. Mason, University of Iowa	$1,139,705
Michael A. McRobbie, Indiana University at Bloomington	$1,111,924

Source: The Chronicle of Higher Education

Highest Paid Private College Presidents in 2011	
Robert J. Zimmer, University of Chicago	$3,358,723
Joseph E. Aoun, Northeastern University	$3,121,864
Dennis J. Murray, Marist College	$2,688,148
Lee C. Bollinger, Columbia University	$2,327,344
Lawrence S. Bacow, Tufts University	$1,223,752
Amy Gutmann, University of Pennsylvania	$1,091,764
Anthony J. Catanese, Florida Institute of Technology	$1,884,008

Source: The Chronicle of Higher Education

Preparation and Recommendations

The survey also addressed leadership programs that may have strengthened administrators' skills. There are five leadership programs mentioned in this research: Kellogg NAFEO MSI Leadership Program, Executive Leadership Summit (ELS), Millennium Leadership Initiative (MLI), American Council on Education Fellows Program (ACE), and Harvard Institutes for Higher Education (HIHE). The Kellogg NAFEO Program and the Executive Leadership Summit, however, are discussed at length. Individuals were asked to list other leadership programs in which they had participated.

Table 3. Institution Affiliation by Leadership Program						
Affiliation	Number	ACE	Kellogg/NAFEO	MLI	HIHE	Other
HBCU	12	1	4	2	5	5
PWI	8	2	1	2	3	-
Totals	20	3	4	3	7	8

Source: The Chronicle of Higher Education

Kellogg NAFEO MSI Leadership Program

The Kellogg NAFEO MSI Leadership Program is one of the newly established programs that address the needs of minority serving institutions. The inaugural class began in 2003–2004 for three types of minority serving institutions: National Association for Equal Opportunity in Higher Education (NAFEO), American Indian Higher Education Consortium (AIHEC), and Hispanic Association of Colleges and Universities (HACU). Many of the presidents, particularly those who had retired, stated that they needed or wanted someone who was ready to step into the presidency and move the agenda forward. It was also stated that many individuals who had become new presidents did not have the preparation, knowledge or experience to lead an HBCU. The Kellogg NAFEO Fellows Program, therefore, is greatly needed to provide our future presidents and other senior-level administrators with the tools needed to succeed in an African American leadership role.

Overall, the program was designed to prepare ten exemplary individuals per year (or thirty individuals across the three programs) for the challenges and rigors of becoming the next generation of senior-level leaders at nearly 340 Minority-Serving Institutions (MSIs) in the United States. In addition to participation in joint and individual workshops, seminars, and discussion groups during the academic year, each Fellow is matched with a Mentor president from another MSI who serves as a guide and resource throughout the Fellowship year and beyond. Mentoring is greatly needed in this field to guide those who aspire to such prestigious positions, as president or provost.

It is important to note that the individual workshops, seminars, and discussion groups focused on the specific type of university. For example, the NAFEO group dealt specifically with issues plaguing HBCUs. This kind of approach is most beneficial to Fellows because minority-serving institutions have distinctive issues compared with PWIs, and even other colleges and universities when one considers the cultural differences. The Kellogg NAFEO Fellows meet head on the challenges that they face in HBCUs, such as a highly restricted budget or the lack of respect and recognition they receive compared to PWIs. Fellows gain invaluable experience from listening and interacting with current model presidents as well as retired presidents. It is equally important to note that the Fellows learn from leaders from such diverse kinds of HBCUs as public and private institutions. Experiences like these are important to enable individuals to lead various kinds of institutions and to ensure that administrators are prepared to deal with various situations they may face at any HBCU.

Executive Leadership Summit

Another fairly new leadership program to address the issues of African American administrators began in 2001: the Executive Leadership Summit (ELS), held at Hampton University. The program was primarily started by William Harvey and known as the "Harvey Executive Leadership Model" to train individuals for administrative positions. It is a two-day workshop that prepares individuals for many kinds of administrative experiences. "The Summit provides participants with an opportunity to receive professional development training from a cadre of highly successful executive leaders through stimulating lectures, case studies, interactive sessions and one-on-one dialogue" (*Chronicle of Higher Education,* Oct. 1, 2004, p. A51). The program is for "presidents (recently appointed), chancellors (recently appointed), provosts, assistant provosts, vice presidents, deans, assistant deans and other appointed executives" (*Chronicle of Higher Education,* Oct. 1, 2004, p. A51). The mission and vision of the summit is to:

- Foster team-building and sharing of knowledge, skills, and abilities between those who hold executive positions and those who aspire to assume top leadership positions;

- Create a network among those serving in the position of president at diverse small and mid-sized comprehensive universities and colleges with emphasis on the challenges presidents face in such settings;
- Provide opportunities for aspiring executive officers to hear first-hand those challenges that presidents face as well as to be exposed to the range of strategies that current leaders have found successful;
- Assist tomorrow's leaders in the development of strategies for accomplishing personal and professional goals; and
- Provide professional development and retooling for those who aspire to maintain excellence in their current leadership positions. (Executive Leadership Summit, 2004)

Presidents who have served under Harvey's leadership return to the campus to share their experiences with current and prospective administrators. The participants who took part in leadership programs believed that the sessions were very beneficial. Among the responses:

- I gained greater insights into the role and scope of community college presidents. The experience and the networking opportunities helped me crystallize my interest in becoming a president.
- The experiences encountered by past chancellors have been very beneficial. They told real stories and how situations were handled.
- The program provided insight and networking opportunities.
- The programs have been beneficial, both personally and professionally, and viewed as significant learning opportunities.
- Actually, building a network of colleagues in specialized disciplines was most beneficial. But, the programs also focused on the principles and "how-to's" of basic leadership and management skills.
- The programs were designed to prepare change agents.
- The Program provided a framework for effective leadership behavior.
- All of the programs have been beneficial.
- The program provided interaction and discussion with other leaders.
- ACE was very instrumental in helping me to develop a clear understanding of transformational change in higher education institutions and the impact of public policy and opinions on the change process.

American Council on Education Fellows Program

The American Council on Education (ACE) Fellows Program has been in existence since 1965. This leadership development program has groomed countless individuals for success in senior-level administrator positions. ACE fellows have the luxury of spending time with a president and witnessing first-hand the routine of a university other than their own. They have an opportunity to observe the university's positive attributes, participate in meetings and seminars, and glean useful take-away ideas. Through completing projects, they gain hands-on experience. They also build a solid network of administrators who can serve as a sounding board for ideas and questions that may arise regarding upper-level administration. Many members of their network will be encountered during a required three-week seminar.

Becoming an ACE Fellow requires the nomination of the president or chief academic officer of one's institution. The nominator is required to pay the Fellow's salary as well as benefits for the duration of the program. There is a screening process in which the nominees must have leadership experience as a vice president, department chair, director of admissions, and so on. The fellow and the nominator select the institution in which the Fellow will serve his or her one-year term.

Millennium Leadership Initiative

This program is specifically geared toward underrepresented minority groups of administrators striving for presidency at a university. There are two components to the program: the mentor component and the protégé. There is a four-day conference that consists of sessions, seminars, and lectures that are meant to prepare the participants for leadership positions in higher education. Immediately following the completion of this program, each participant is then assigned a current or former president or chancellor to serve as a mentor. The MLI program firmly believes in pairing everyone with a mentor to help guide him or her through any issues that may arise during or even after the completion of the program. The mentor assists the protégé in career evaluation exercises while aiding the mentee in laying out a precise and accurate career plan to achieve the career goals set forth by the protégé. Each mentor provides an evaluation of the experience as well as the protégé they were paired with to the director of the MLI.

Harvard Institute for Higher Education

The Harvard Institute for Higher Education is more similar to ACE than the other programs previously discussed. HIHE is not specifically geared toward minorities; however, it does have specific sectors that are geared toward underrepresented groups. The main objective of the program is to "attract educational leaders who bring a commitment to personal growth and institutional success." The HIHE also consists of a wide array of conferences, seminars, lectures, and so forth, most of which are carried out over a span of a week or two. Each program has its own unique target audience. Some programs are target to administrators with three to seven years of experience; some go all the way up to ten or more years of experience. Each program is designed for its target audience and covers issues that administrators typically face during those time spans.

HIHE is one of the most well-respected higher education preparation programs in the county. It has great ties within both the educational and business realms. The program recruits individuals from all sorts of backgrounds because our world is becoming more and more diverse each day, particularly the world of higher education.

As illustrated in the responses, the Kellogg NAFEO MSI Leadership Program and the Executive Leadership Summit have helped to sharpen participants' skills and have helped them serve as better leaders, enabling them to take their colleges and universities to the next level. This is not to say that the Millennium Leadership Initiative, American Council on Education Fellows Program, Harvard Institutes for Higher Education, or any other professional conferences and programs geared toward higher education are poor programs. They have certainly aided many senior-level administrators and aspiring senior-level administrators in their efforts to increase their knowledge and skills at their respective universities.

References

ABC News website. (2009). Gunfire Breaks Out on Texas Southern University Campus Injuring 8. Retrieved November 10, 2013, from http://abcnews.go.com/US/story?id=8160368

ABC News website. (2012). Virginia Tech shooting fine overturned by Department of Education. Retrieved November 10, 2013, from http://www.wjla.com/articles/2012/03/virginia-tech-shooting-fine-overturned-by-department-of-education-74383.html

Alpha Delta Chi Delta Chapter v. Charles Reed, 9th Circuit (2011).

Aronwitz, S. (1998). *Post-Work: Wages of Cybernation.* Taylor and Francis: London.

Atkinson, R.C. (1968). Computerized instruction and the learning process. *American Psychologist*, 23(4), 225–239.

Bodah, M. (2000). Significant labor and employment law issues in higher education during the past decade and what to look for now: the perspective of an academician; *Journal of Law in Education,* 29: 317.

Branch, T. (2011). The Shame of College Sports. *The Atlantic*

Brown, R. (2012). Alabama: Ex-professor gets life term in shooting. *New York Times*

Cardinal Points Online website. (2007). Former PSUC president involved in censorship issue. Retrieved November 4, 2013, from http://www.cardinalpointsonline.com/news/former-psuc-president-involved-in-censorship-issue-1.781369#.Un_S8OKh4lI

Center for National Education Statistics (2012-2013) Report on Student Enrolled in American Colleges and Universities.

Choate-Nielsen, A (2012) Religion on Campus: Status of Religious Student Groups is Challenged by Court Ruling. *Deseret News*

Christian Legal Society, *Chapter of University of California Hastings College of Law v. Martinez* (No. 08-1371) 319 Fed. Appx. 645.

Chronicle website. (2007). *Parents are awarded $1.5-million in hazing death of SUNY-Plattsburgh student.* Retrieved November 9, 2013, from http://chronicle.com/article/Parents-Are-Awarded/40069

Clarke, M., & Fine, G. A. (2010). " A" for apology: slavery and the discourse of remonstrance in two American universities. *History & Memory, 22*(1), 81–112.

Claflin University website. (2011). *The Campaign for Claflin University.* Retrieved January 21, 2014, from http://issuu.com/sonjaab/docs/cu_new_case_final_62_revised_2?e=4293052/2745598

Cohen, A.M. (1998). *The Shaping of American Higher Education: Emergence and Growth of the Contemporary System.* San Francisco: Jossey-Bass.

College Media Matters website. (2012). Kansas Student Body President: Cut Daily Kansan's Funding. Retrieved November 9, 2013, from http://www.collegeme diamatters.com/2010/03/11/kansas-student-body-president-time-to-cut-ties-with-daily-kansan/

College Media Matters website. (2013). America's oldest college newspaper? At least 8 papers claim the title (Sort of). Retrieved November 5, 2013, from http://www.collegemediamatters.com/2013/09/18/americas-oldest-college-newspaper-at-least-8-papers-claim-the-title-sort-of/

Council for Aid to Education website. (2013). Colleges and Universities Raise $31 Billion in 2012. 2.3 percent increase only slightly ahead of inflation. Retrieved January 5, 2014, from http://cae.org/fundraising-in-education/category/annual-press-release/

Crowley, J.N. (1994). *No Equal in the World: An Interpretation of the Academic Presidency.* Reno, NV: University of Nevada Press.

Cruz, G. (2008). A brief history of: the GI Bill. *Times Magazine*

Family Educational Rights and Privacy Act, FERPA (1974) (20 U.S.C. § 1232g; 34 CFR Part 99).

Fauntroy, M.K. (2008) *Republicans and the Black Vote.* Boulder, CO: Lynne Rienner Publishers.

Firmin, M. W., & Firebaugh, S. (2008). Historical Analysis of College Campus Interracial Dating. *College Student Journal, 42*(3).

Fishman, S.B. (2000) *Jewish Life and American Culture.* New York, NY: University of New York Press.

French, D. (2005) Victory for Religious Freedom at Louisiana State University. Retrieved May 22, 2014, from http://www.thefire.org/victory-for-religious-freedom-at-louisiana-state-university/

Goodchild, L.F.; Lovell, C.D.; Hines, E.R.; Gill, J.I. (1997). *Public Policy and Higher Education.* ASHE Reader Series. Needham Heights, MA: Pearson Custom Publishing.

Graysgreen, A. (2011) Race at Alabama. *Inside Higher Ed*

Hopkins, K. (2012). International Students Continue to Flock to U.S. Colleges, Grad Schools The probability of having to pay the brunt of costs did not dampen enrollment numbers in 2011–2012. *U.S. News & World Report*

Inside Higher Ed website. (2012). Education Department and Yale Settle Title IX Complaint. Retrieved November 8, 2013, from http://www.insidehighered.com/quicktakes/2012/06/18/education-department-and-yale-settle-title-ix-complaint

Inside Higher Ed website. (2012). The Other Debt Crisis. Retrieved February 3, 2014, from http://www.insidehighered.com/news/2012/04/10/public-universities-will-take-more-debt-states-decrease-spending-capital-projects

Inside Higher Ed website. (2010).What the Alumni Read (or Ignore). Retrieved June 16, 2012, from http://www.insidehighered.com/news/2010/07/09/alumni

Ionescu, A (2012). New e-learning method using databases. *Database Systems Journal, 3*(3), 35.

Julius, D & Gumport, P. (2002). Graduate student unionization: catalysts and consequences, *Review of Higher Education*, 26(2): 187–216.

Leon, D.J. (Eds.). (2005). *Lessons in Leadership: Executive Leadership Programs for Advancing Diversity in Higher Education*. Oxford, UK: Elsevier, Ltd.

Lisby, G.C. (2002). Resolving the hazelwood conundrum: The first amendment rights of college students in kincaid v. gibson and beyond. *Communication Law and Policy*, 7(2).

Marklin, M.B. (2011) More foreign students studying in the USA. *USA Today*.

Mays, B.E. (2003) *Born to Rebel*. Athens, GA: University of Georgia Press.

National Public Radio (2012) Bowie State Boasts First Black LGBT Student Center. Interview with Michael Martin, June 14, 2012.

Nondiscrimination on the Basis of Sex in Education Programs, Title IX (1972) (20 U.S.C. 1681, etseq.)

Porter, E. W. (1972) The Bassett affair: something to remember. *South Atlantic Quarterly*, 72, 451–460.

Rhoads, R. & Rhoades, G. (2005). Graduate employee unionization as symbol of and challenge to the corporatization of U.S. research universities, *The Journal of Higher Education*, 76(3): 243–275.

Rose, D. (2010). Title IX has fought gender discrimination on campuses for forty years. *The Progressive*

Schreiner, B. (2011) Kentucky Prof Retiring After Slavery Remark to Student. *The Huffington Post*

Severson, K. (2011). University provost is sued over faculty shootings. *New York Times*

Shekleton, J.F. (2009). Strangers at the Gate: Academic Autonomy, Civil Rights, Civil Liberties, and Unfinished Tasks, *Journal of College and University Law*, 36: 875.

Smith, R.A. (1988). *Sports in Freedom: The Rise of Big Time College Athletics*. New York, NY: Oxford University Press

Smith, R.A. (2011). *Pay for Play: A History of Big Time College Athletic Reform*. Champaign, IL: University of Illinois Press

The Journal of Blacks in Higher Education (n.d.) Bob Jones University Apologizes for its Racist Past

The Knight Report. (2009). An overview of the business and economic landscape of intercollegiate athletics.

Thelin, J.R. (2011) A *History of American Higher Education*, Second Edition. Baltimore, MD: Johns Hopkins University Press.

Thrash, R. (2007). Victim of hazing saw no way out. *Tampa Bay Times*

Tucker, S. (2001). Distance education: Better, worse, or as good as traditional education? *Online Journal of Distance Learning Administration, 4*(4).

U.S. Department of Education, National Center for Education Statistics (NCES) website. (2011). *Digest of Education Statistics, 2011* (NCES 2012-001), Chapter 3. Retrieved on October 29, 2013, from, http://nces.ed.gov/fastfacts/display.asp?id=98.

U.S. Department of Defense website. (2013). GI Bill Transferability Has Arrived. Retrieved on November 2, 2013, from http://www.defense.gov/home/features/2009/0409_gibill/

USA Today (2011-2012) College Basketball Coach Salary Database. *Forbes*

USA Today (2006-2011) College Football Coach Salary Database

Voice of America website. (2013). Virginia Governor Forms Panel to Probe College Massacre. Retrieved November 10, 2013, from http://www.voanews.com/content/a-13-2007-04-20-voa11/347840.html

Wilder, C. (2012) Ebony *and Ivy. Ebony and Ivy: Race, Slavery, and the Troubled History of America's Universities.* New York, NY: Bloomsbury Press.

Winerip, M. (2012). When Hazing Goes Very Wrong. *New York Times*

Wright, L. (1999). The stonewall riots—1969. *Socialism Today, 40.*

Yale University (The Graduate School of Arts and Sciences) website. (2013). Within the Yale University website. Retrieved July 9, 2013, from http://www.yale.edu/printer/bulletin/htmlfiles/grad/the-graduate-school-of-arts-and-sciences.html

Index